A Pictorial World History

BOOK THREE

W.H. Ha
Principal, St. Paul's College

C.L.J. Hallward
History Mistress,
St. Stephen's Girls' College

LONGMAN

LONGMAN GROUP (FAR EAST) LIMITED
Quarry Bay, Hong Kong

LONGMAN GROUP LIMITED
London

*Associated companies, branches and representatives
throughout the world*

© Longman Group Ltd 1973

*First published *1973*

ISBN 0 582 67041 1

Set in 'Monophoto' Univers 689 11 on 12 pt.

*Typeset in Hong Kong
by Asco Trade Typesetting Ltd
Printed in Hong Kong
by Sheck Wah Tong Printing Press*

Contents

Colour plates appear on pages 13, 14, 31–34, 51, 52,
69–72, 105, 106, 139, 140.

ACKNOWLEDGEMENTS

For permission to reproduce the photographs on the pages mentioned below, the publishers are grateful to the following:

Monochrome: Aerofilms for page 79; Archiv Gerstenberg for page 110; Arts Council for page 55; Australian News and Information Bureau for page 59 (right); Bluett and Sons for page 103; British Museum for pages 22 (bottom), 85 (left), 102, 109, 111 (bottom); Camera Press for pages 1, 62 (right), 63, 77 (both), 80, 83 (top left and bottom left), 95 (left), 98 (both), 116 (top), 117, 119, 122 (both), 124 (both), 129 (both), 130 (bottom), 131 (top), 133, 135 (both); Confederation Life Collection for page 58 (right); Crown Copyright for page 43; J.R. Freeman for pages 9 (top), 21 (bottom), 27 (top), 44, 48 (bottom), 50 (bottom left), 54 (right), 61 (right), 87, 90, 108 (both); Giraudon for page 22 (top); Japanese Embassy for page 123; A.F. Kersting for page 53 (top); Keystone Press for pages 130 (top), 131 (bottom), 132; Mansell Collection for pages 3 (both), 4, 10, 25, 28 (top), 29, 30, 35 (bottom right), 36, 41, 42, 45 (bottom), 47 (top), 58 (top), 59 (left), 62 (left), 68 (both), 74, 81 (bottom), 86 (bottom), 88, 93 (top), 96, 113, 126, 137 (bottom), 138; Museum of Modern Art, New York for page 137 (top); National Monuments Record for pages 53 (bottom left and bottom right); National Portrait Gallery for pages 26, 45 (top), 95 (right); New York Historical Society for page 65; Novosti Press Agency for pages 112, 128; Penguin Books for pages 18 (both), 19, 114; Popperfoto for pages 97, 127; Radio Times Hulton Picture Library for pages 9 (bottom), 27 (bottom left), 28 (bottom), 35 (top right), 37, 38, 40, 46 (both), 49, 50 (bottom right), 60 (right), 66 (both), 73, 78, 89 (left), 94, 100, 134 (middle and bottom); Roger-Viollet for pages 39, 50 (top left), 83 (right); Science Museum for page 134 (top); Victoria and Albert Museum for pages 20, 27 (bottom right), 48 (top) and Weidenfeld and Nicolson for pages 15, 16 (both), 17 (top), 21 (top), 23, 75, 81 (top), 86 (top), 89 (right), 107, 115, 116 (bottom) and 118.

All other pictures are from the authors' or publishers' collections.

Colour: The Bodleian Library for page 32 (bottom), MS Douce 363 f47; Jane Dorner for page 139 (top right and top left); Giraudon for pages 32 (top), 33 (top and bottom left), 34 (both); J.R. Freeman and the Victoria and Albert Museum for page 51 (top); Michael Holford Library for page 71 (both); Michael Holford Library and the British Museum for page 14 (top); Michael Holford Library and Count Brobinskoy for page. 33 (bottom right); Michael Holford Library and the Courtauld Institute, London for page 52 (bottom left); Michael Holford Library and the Fitzwilliam Museum for page 52 (top); Michael Holford Library and Lady Hulton for page 140 (top); Michael Holford Library and the Louvre for page 52 (bottom right); Michael Holford Library and the Musée Guimet, Paris for page 106 (top); Michael Holford Library and the National Gallery for page 51 (bottom); Michael Holford Library and the National Maritime Museum for pages 69 (top) and 72 (top); Michael Holford Library and the Royal Geographical Society for page 70 (top); Michael Holford Library and the Victoria and Albert Museum for pages 13 (top left, top right and bottom right), 14 (bottom), 105 (bottom); the Japanese Embassy for page 106 (bottom); the National Portrait Gallery for page 31; Picturepoint Ltd for page 139 (bottom); the Royal Army Museum for page 105 (top); the Sunday Times for page 72 (bottom); the Tate Gallery for page 140 (bottom); the Victoria and Albert Museum for page 13 (bottom left); Weidenfeld & Nicolson for pages 69 (bottom), 70 (bottom).

1
China – the Ming and Yüan Dynasties

Rise of the Border Peoples

From earliest times, Chinese rulers were faced with the problem of dealing with the peoples lying just beyond the borders. These peoples lived in less fertile areas, in the deserts, plains and grasslands of the Asian continent. They were fierce, hardy people who boasted that they were descended from mythical animals. They lived in round felt tents called yurts, moving here and there to pasture their flocks of horses, cattle and sheep and to grow their millet. They were natural horsemen and were used to fighting, because they lived partly by plundering from other tribes. The strongest tribes moved nearer and nearer towards the richer farming areas within China, until they had occupied many parts of northern China. During late Sung times, when leadership was weak, this was becoming an increasing problem for setting up armed garrisons of soldiers along the frontiers, and when even this proved unsuccessful they tried to put off the border tribes with regular gifts called tributes.

In the tenth century, a tribe of fierce nomads from Mongolia and Manchuria captured cities in northern China. As their power grew, they founded a dynasty and gave it the Chinese name Liao (遼). They fought an exhausting war with the Sung lasting from A.D. 986 to 1005 when they finally settled down to an uneasy peace. The Chinese promised to pay the Liao a regular annual tribute of 200 000 taels of silver and 300 000 bolts of silk. In return the Liao promised to stay where they were and not advance further. The Sung rulers looked upon this not as falling under the rule of the Liao but rather as a convenient way of buying peace.

This state of affairs did not last very long, however, because another tribe had risen in the north. This tribe came from the eastern part of Manchuria, a land of deep valleys and high mountains. They lived mainly by fishing and hunting in the forests but also farmed in the valleys. At first this tribe paid tribute to the Liao rulers, but encouraged by the Sung, they revolted and destroyed the Liao. They founded the house of the Chin (金) in 1122. The Sung rulers then began to realise that they had underestimated the Chin because they turned out to be more ambitious than the Liao. They even captured the Sung capital of Kaifeng (開封), and pushed the Sung south towards the Yangtze valley. In the end the Southern Sung, as it had now come to be called, had to buy the Chin off by paying regular tribute.

The Liao and the Chin were the more important border peoples who took advantage of the temporary decline of Chinese power to extend their own territories. There were quite a few others who wanted to do the same. Thus, when the Mongols rose from the steppe-land in the northwest in the thirteenth century, they followed roughly the pattern set by the Liao and the Chin before them.

Mongolian yurts

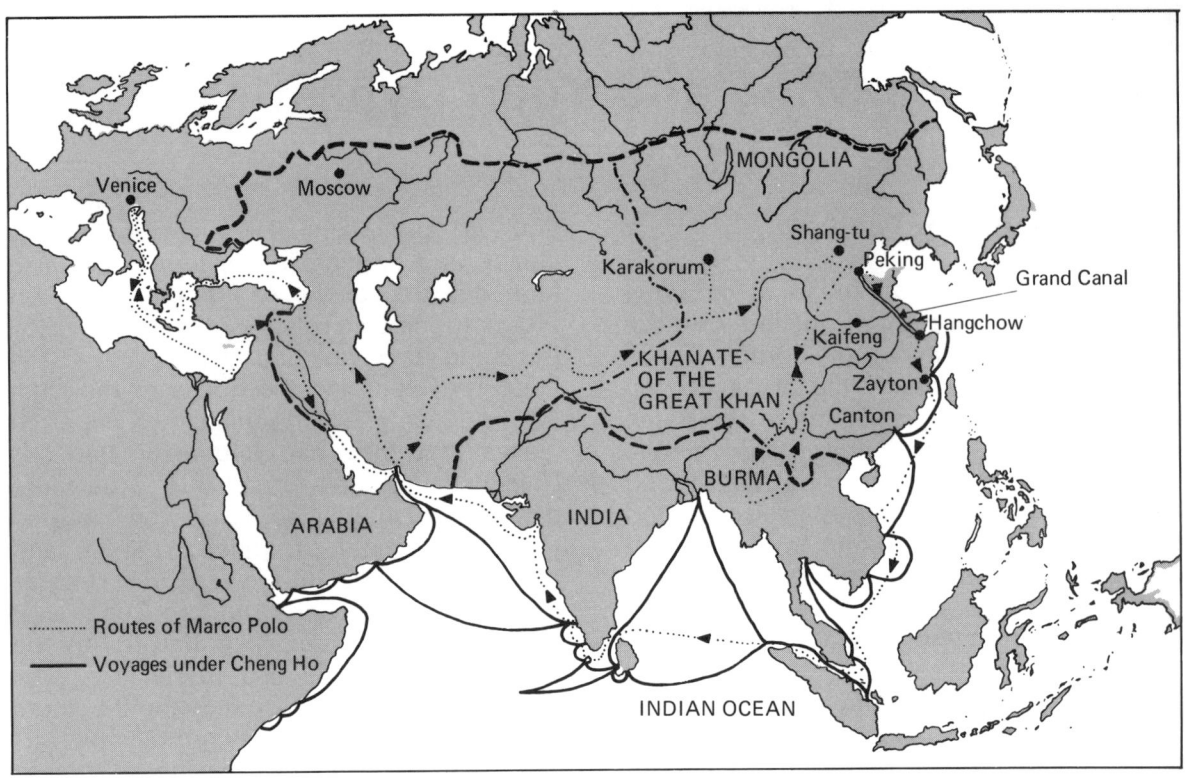

The Mongol empire

Genghis Khan (成吉斯汗)

The leader who united the widely scattered nomads of the region now called Mongolia and set up an empire larger than any in human history was called Temüjin (鐵木眞). Temüjin's father, who ruled several Mongol tribes, was killed when Temujin was still a boy. But Temüjin was determined to show that, young as he was, he was now a tribal chief. He was a good general and an able and cunning politician. By playing off one chief against another, he gradually gathered a large number of Mongol tribes under him. At a grand conference of the chiefs held in 1206 on the Kerulen River, a tributary of the Amur, he was elected leader of all the chiefs. He was then forty-four years old. He took the title of Genghis Khan, which meant Universal Ruler or Chief of Chiefs. (Khan is a word of Turkish origin meaning lord or prince.) He chose Karakorum as his capital.

Once firmly in control, Genghis Khan began to make plans to extend his rule further afield. But first he had to settle affairs at home. As the Mongols had no writing of their own he gave orders that they should learn the Turkish script, which came from the ancient Phoenician alphabet. This is why so many Mongolian names are known to us today in their Turkish form. He also tried to stabilise the laws because the Mongols were a rough and lawless people and he had to show his authority. He collected all the law codes of the Mongol tribes and made them into a new law code of the empire called the Great Yasa.

Genghis picked able sons of chiefs and generals as his own personal Imperial Guard. Once chosen, they were trained under very strict discipline. Then he would appoint his generals and high officials from their ranks. This loyal and well-trained group of leaders enabled the khan to keep the empire under close control.

Genghis was an ambitious ruler. He had been dreaming of world conquest from boyhood. He is believed to have said: 'The greatest joy of man is to win victories, to conquer his enemies, to chase them, to take away their belongings, to make their loved ones weep, to ride on their horses and to

Genghis Khan

take their wives and daughters.' Before his death he had extended his control from Korea and northern China in the East to northern India, Persia and south-eastern Europe in the West. The secret of Mongol power was its fierce cavalry. His horse-soldiers were dressed in animal skins. They were so hardy that they could live on horse-back several days and nights on end. In battle they would hold plenty of fresh horses in reserve. They used long powerful bows and arrows with armour-piercing steel heads. Coloured flags and lights were used as signals, and spies were sent out ahead to gather information or to spread rumours. Whole towns — men, women and children — were often killed on purpose to put fear into the hearts of their next victims.

Kublai Khan (忽必烈汗)

Genghis Khan died in 1227 while actively directing his troops in campaigns in northern China. After his death, the empire was divided into four main areas of rule called khanates. The most important was the khanate of the Great Khan made up of Mongolia and northern China. At first the Southern Sung allied with the Mongols to fight the Chin. But when Chin power was destroyed, the Mongols turned against their ally. For the Mongols the conquest of southern China was not an easy task. It took more than a generation to complete. Gradually the horse-riding Mongols mastered the skill of seige warfare against the walled cities of the south. Gigantic catapults, each manned by as many as a hundred soldiers, hurled rocks or explosive bombs over long distances. Very simple wooden cannons which used gunpowder were also employed.

The conquest of the Southern Sung was finally completed by Genghis Khan's grandson, Kublai Khan who was born in 1215. His forces chased the last descendant of the royal house to the Kowloon Peninsula opposite what is today Hong Kong island. There the boy was killed when his faithful follower carrying him in his arms jumped off a cliff into the sea, to save him from capture.

Even before this, Kublai had declared a new dynasty in China called the Yüan (元), meaning the 'Beginning' in 1271. Marco Polo whom we read about in Book Two wrote of Kublai Khan: 'He is a man of good stature, neither short nor tall but of moderate height. His limbs are well fleshed out and modelled in due proportion. His complexion is fair and ruddy like a rose. The eyes black and handsome, the nose shapely and set squarely in place.' Kublai's reign was a long one. He did not rule as a rough Mongol chief but as a civilised emperor in the Chinese style. Because of the importance of China, he moved his capital from Karakorum to Cambaluc (Khan-balik, the khan's city) which was the site of modern Peking. Mongol power reached its highest point under the leadership of Kublai Khan.

Kublai Khan hunting with an eagle

Rule of the Yüan

The Mongol conquerors brought with them a way of life which was quite different from that of the Chinese of the more settled areas. The Mongols were used to the rough life of the steppes and the desert. The Chinese thought they were uncivilised and barbaric. On the whole the Mongols failed to prove to the conquered Chinese that their intentions were good, so they always had to be on their guard in case rebellions broke out. Even Marco Polo, writing from his own observation, said that this could happen at any time. The Mongols stationed strong garrisons at various points of the country to guard against this.

Partly owing to the distrust of the Chinese, the Yüan emperor employed many foreigners in his government, especially Muslims from inland Asia; they came from the Tartar and Saracen tribes. There were also quite a number of Christians in the government, and Chinese officials were also employed. Examinations were held from time to time to select the best scholars but they hardly ever received any jobs higher than clerical. The Mongols were also allowed to follow a different and more lenient set of laws than the Chinese. The population of the whole empire was divided into clearly separated classes. The Mongols were the most privileged class; they were followed by the non-Chinese supporters of the Yüan dynasty; then came the Chinese of northern China while the Chinese of the south had the fewest rights. This was because they had resisted the Mongols under the Southern Sung. For a short time, these measures succeeded in strengthening the rule of the Mongols.

Marco Polo

The great extent of the territory under the control of the Mongols made it easy for travellers to move from one place to another across the continent. Two merchant brothers, Maffeo and Niccolo Polo brought Maffeo's son, Marco, with them on their second journey from the prosperous Italian city of Venice to China. This country was then known to them as Cathay, a word of Turkish origin. The brothers had visited China before and had met Kublai Khan. They were asked to invite the Pope to send one hundred Christian scholars to China. This did not prove possible but the Khan still received the brothers warmly.

The Polo brothers are entertained to dinner at the court of Kublai Khan

A boat on the Grand Canal

The young Marco, only seventeen years old, entered the Khan's service as an official in the department controlling the production and sale of salt. In the course of his duties, he made many trips through the country. He learnt to speak Mongol, Turkish and Persian easily and so could move from place to place. When he eventually returned to Venice, after spending seventeen years (1275–1292) in the khan's service, few believed the stories he told about the splendours of Cathay. Later as a prisoner-of-war in the rival city of Genoa, he spent his time in prison dictating a book about his travels called *Description of the World*.

Marco Polo was not the only European who travelled in China but he had the most extensive experience and was the only one who has left a reliable written record. His book has been translated into many languages, and his travels have been traced and confirmed by scholars. His book inspired countless European travellers. Even Columbus was said to have a well-thumbed copy of the book always by his side and the stories he read about the East made him determined to visit it. Our knowledge of Yüan China has also been greatly enriched by Marco Polo's tales.

Life under the Mongols

Life under the Mongols was reasonably prosperous; trade was active; for the first time paper money was widely used and was accepted from Korea to South-east Asia; transport was improved too. To move the grain from the more fertile south to the north, the old Grand Canal was extended from Hangchow (杭州) to Cambaluc, which was a distance of over 1 000 miles. Marco Polo reports 'it is equally possible to go by land, for alongside the waterway there runs a causeway'.

Overseas trade with India and South-east Asia also flourished. The port of Ch'üan-chou (泉州), better known by its Arab name of Zayton, became the centre of this trade. Marco Polo writes: 'Zayton is the port for all ships that arrive from India laden with costly wares and precious stones of great price and big pearls of fine quality', and 'for one spice ship that goes to Alexandria or elsewhere, to pick up pepper for export to Christendom (Europe), Zayton is visited by a hundred.' This trade brought cultural benefits too. Arab and Persian merchants brought with them teachers of astronomy, ceramics and mathematics. The Chinese gave the

Arabs, and through them the Europeans, a knowledge of gunpowder, paper, printed money and fine products like porcelain and silk.

Chinese porcelain had been admired outside China for many centuries. In Yüan times, the secret of the art was passed on and developed. Marco Polo notes with admiration the great care given to the clay used in the making of porcelain:

'These dishes are made of crumbly earth or clay which is dug as though from a mine and stacked in huge mounds and then left for thirty or forty years exposed to wind, rain and sun...when a man makes a mound of this earth, he does so for his children; the time of maturing is so long that he cannot hope to draw any profit from it himself.'

Marco Polo also made very interesting observations on the two great cities of the

A porcelain kiln

窰器瓷

Yüan empire, Cambaluc in the north and Hangchow, the old Southern Sung capital, in the south. Cambaluc was surrounded by a square city wall, each side being a mile in length. It had a thick wall of fully ten paces in height.

He writes of the khan's palace in the city:

'The khan's palace has a very high roof. Inside, the walls of the halls and chambers are all covered with gold and silver and decorated with pictures of dragons and birds and horsemen and various breeds of beasts and scenes of battles... the hall is so vast and so wide that a meal might well be served there for 6 000 men. [After a dinner given by the khan] the tables are removed, a great troupe of jugglers and acrobats and entertainers comes into the hall and performs remarkable feats of various kinds.'

All this luxury, however, could not disguise the fact that the khan's rule had not been popular. His fortune-tellers or astrologers were always warning him that there might be a great uprising. Even in the capital a strict curfew was observed every night. After the sounding of a bell, 'no one ventures abroad in the city except in case of childbirth or illness, and those who are called out by such emergencies are obliged to carry lights'.

Hangchow in the south was even grander in many ways. Marco Polo calls it the 'City of Heaven' and says 'it is without doubt the finest and most splendid city in the world'. It was a city with numerous crowded market places. There were 12 000 bridges in the city and the main ones were high enough to let big ships pass underneath. The lakes produced great quantities of fish which the Polo brothers found very good. The wives of the richer merchants were 'most refined and angelic creatures, and so adorned with silks and jewellery that their value cannot be counted'. In Hangchow, as in Cambaluc, the khan kept strict watch over the people, more so as he thought the people in the south were less reliable. Every person had to write the names of his family and the number of horses he owned on the door of his house. Those who kept inns were ordered to keep a record of all travellers'

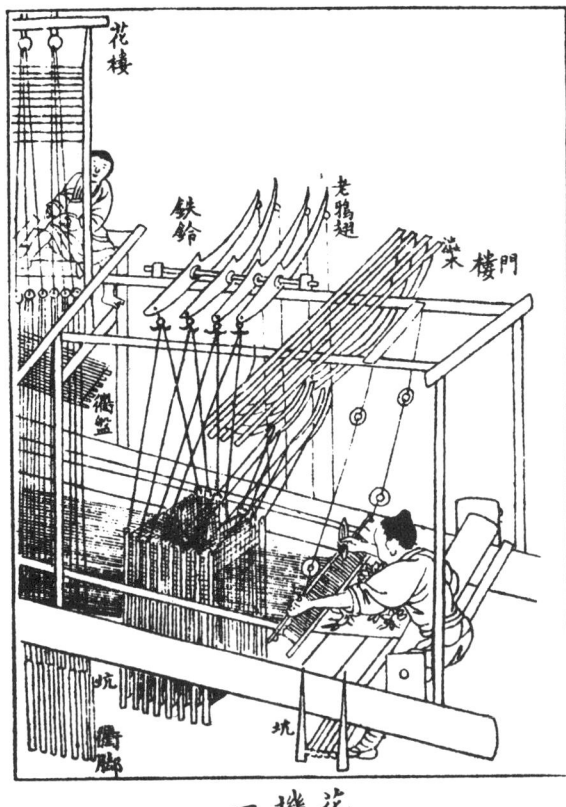

花樓

鐵鈴

老鴉翅

棚門

渦笙

坑

掛腳

坑

一機花

Weaving silk

Kublai Khan died in 1294. None of his successors was as able as he was, and for half a century the Mongol princes quarrelled and fought among themselves. A long period of famine was followed by widespread flooding of the Yellow River. The system Kublai built to control the country began to break down. The Chinese had never accepted Mongol rule and they took this opportunity to rise in revolt.

Chu Yüan-chang (朱元璋)

One of the chief rebels was Chu Yüan-chang, founder of the Ming (明) dynasty. He joined the rebel movement by chance. He was the third son of a family of small farmers. When he was seventeen, a series of misfortunes came to his village in the form of droughts and a plague. To avoid starvation, he joined a neighbouring Buddhist monastery as a monk but even the monastery was too poor and when there was no more food the monks had to abandon it. Chu had to leave too. He wandered from city to city, begging for a living, and remained a beggar monk for four years before returning to the monastery. These four years, however, were very important years for him. His experiences made him more mature, and he made many useful friends, some of whom were members of secret societies.

Secret societies have a long history in China. Their origins can be traced as far back as the Sung dynasty or even earlier. There were often strong religious connections. The performance of elaborate rites was an important part of their activities. Secret societies had been connected with many uprisings. Marco Polo confirms that the Mongol rulers were very much aware of these activities. When Yüan power became weak, the rebels became even more daring, and Chu joined them. He was then twenty-five.

In spite of his lack of training, Chu proved to be an outstanding general. Gradually he rose from the ranks. After winning a series of campaigns, his name became almost a legend. He first took the Yangtze valley provinces. Then he moved against Cambaluc.

names and the length of their stay. Guards patrolled the city by night and a strong garrison was stationed just outside the city gates.

Marco Polo admired the young ladies of China and wrote:

'They do not keep watch at the windows gazing at passers-by or exposing themselves to their gaze. They do not listen to improper stories. They do not gad about to parties and entertainments. If it happens that they go out to some respectable place, as for instance to the temples of their idols or to visit the houses of relatives, they walk in the company of their mothers, not glancing brazenly about them, but some of them wear pretty hoods over their heads . . . On their way they always walk with their eyes cast down in front of their feet. In the presence of their elders they are respectful and never utter a needless word — indeed they do not speak at all in their presence unless addressed.'

Yüan rule was weakened by years of internal quarrels among rival members of the royal family and rival generals. When the rebel forces under Chu reached the capital in 1368, the imperial family opened the city gates and fled north.

Earlier in the same year, before Cambaluc was seized, Chu Yüan-chang proclaimed himself emperor of the Ming dynasty. For his capital, he chose Nanking. He took the title, Hung-wu (洪武), which means Great Military Power. Mongol power had still not been completely destroyed but it was no longer a serious threat to the new dynasty.

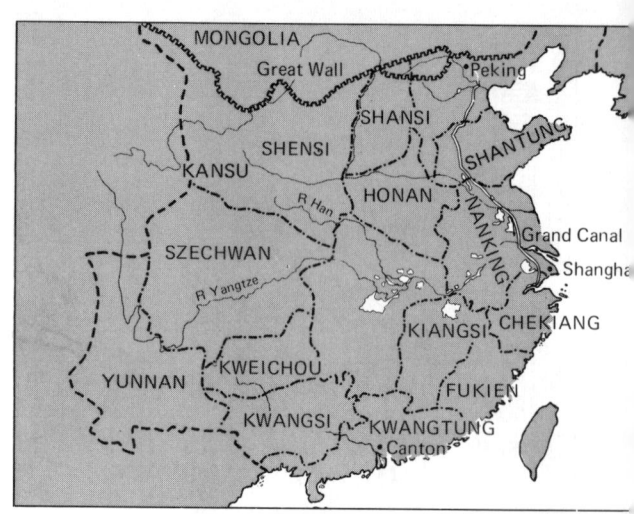

China under the Ming dynasty

Hung-wu (洪武)

Hung-wu received very little formal schooling because of the very disturbed times he lived in. Like many other famous men of action, he had little respect for scholars or book learning, but he nevertheless thought it wise to give official encouragement to scholarship. He built schools where classical Confucian books could be studied. His court observed all rites and ceremonies connected with Confucius. Perhaps Hung-wu felt that the people were tired of foreign rule and it would be wise for him to make known that the new dynasty was a Chinese dynasty founded on time-honoured tradition. The emperor's other measures also followed this thinking. He restored the government on traditional lines. He made a new set of laws based on the T'ang model with only minor alterations. He also followed the old example of selecting his officials from candidates who were successful at civil service examinations.

Yung-lo (永樂)

Hung Wu died at the age of seventy. In 1398 he left his throne to a grandson who was then only sixteen. A struggle began almost immediately between the new emperor and his uncles. The civil war continued for four years. Then his fourth uncle, Chu Ti (朱棣), captured Nanking in 1403. When the city fell the boy emperor disappeared. It was rumoured that he escaped after disguising himself in a monk's cloak, following the example of his grandfather. Chu Ti then became emperor and chose Yung-lo as his title. 'Yung-lo' (永樂) means 'Perpetual Happiness'. During Yung-lo's reign, Ming power was brought to its highest point. None of his successors could claim as great an achievement.

One of the first major decisions Yung-Lo made was to move his capital from Nanking to Peking, but he kept the former as his subsidiary capital. He wanted to make a fresh start by freeing the capital from the influence of forces still remaining loyal to the boy emperor. He was also now better able to direct the campaigns against the Mongols. The imperial Forbidden City in Peking was completely rebuilt on a magnificent scale. Today it stands as a reminder of the splendid achievements of Chinese architects.

Yung-lo continued Hung-wu's policy of giving official support to scholarship and Confucian teaching. His most valuable contribution to the culture of the period was the compilation of the gigantic encyclopaedia known as the *Yung-lo ta-tien* (永樂大典) meaning the Encyclopaedia of the Yung-lo Period. This project was undertaken at his direct orders. Yung-lo felt that, after so many years of Mongol rule and political upheaval, the time had come to collect together what was left of Chinese learning. Over 2 000 scholars worked at it for years. Works on history, geography, literature and various other subjects were carefully collected and copied by hand. The result was a huge work of 11 095 volumes, containing 22 000 chapters. The whole work was put in a special library in the Imperial Academy in the capital. Unfortunately, only four hundred volumes survive today.

Life under Ming Rule

The long peace under the rule of the Ming emperors (1368–1644) brought great advances to the material life of the people. Because of active overseas trade and maritime expeditions people knew much more about the geography of the world. They became aware of the huge extent of the empire and the varied, colourful way of life of people living in different parts. Atlases and geographical books were widely used. The best known was the *I-t'ung chih* (一統誌) or Geography of the Empire published in the fifteenth century. It was so popular that revisions were still made several centuries later. New plants were introduced from overseas. The sweet potato, the peanut, maize and the pineapple came from America. Tobacco was introduced from the Philippines. The population increased rapidly. No accurate census was kept but the population must have reached the hundred million mark. The Grand Canal was deepened and improved and a fleet of over three thousand boats used this waterway.

Improvements were also made in the methods of production. A book published in 1637, called the *T'ien-kung k'ai-wu*, (天工開物) describes the methods used in the processing and planting of rice, the production of silk, the mining of salt, the making of sugar and paper, the production of pottery, the treatment of metals and even such subjects as pearl fishing and explosives making. The abundant woodblock illustrations are especially valuable as they give us a better understanding of the stage of technology reached in China at that

The Forbidden City

A porcelain jar of the Ming dynasty

9

Matteo Ricci

tails of nearly 10000 prescriptions. Even today this work is still regarded as one of the chief references for practising herbal doctors. Modern medical research on Chinese medicine also draws many references from it.

Under Ming rule there was greater religious tolerance and Christian missionaries from Europe were welcomed. We shall read how these men came to the East in Chapter 10. One missionary who came to China was a Jesuit called Matteo Ricci who arrived in China in 1582. He was very interested in the Chinese way of life. He dressed and lived in the Chinese manner and studied Confucian books. The Chinese found that they could learn much from him, especially in mathematics and astronomy. Ricci lived in China for twenty-eight years spreading Jesuit teachings. When he died in Peking in 1610 he had gained great influence and many high officials at the court of the emperor became Christians.

Cheng Ho's Voyages

Soon after Hung-wu became emperor, goodwill missions were sent to China's many neighbours informing them of the change in government. The missions were also told to invite the rulers of these states to come to China. States like Japan, Korea, the Liu-chius, Annam, Champa, Malacca, Java and Sumatra were all invited. Many of these states did send return missions to China; when they arrived the emperor presented them with even larger gifts than the tributes they brought. Members of the missions were also permitted to do private trading in Chinese cities *en route*. This has been called the 'tribute system' of foreign relations. Later, it was even found necessary to keep open the three major ports in Southern China, Ch'üan-chou, Ningpo (寧波) and Canton (廣州) for this purpose.

Yung-lo carried this policy even further. He and his successors despatched great sea expeditions to countries in the 'Western Oceans', meaning South-east Asia. The leader of seven of these expeditions was a court eunuch called Cheng Ho (鄭和).

time. Indeed some scholars think that China could well have become an industrial nation before countries in Europe if the Ming dynasty had not fallen in the seventeenth century.

Another scientific classic was also compiled in this period. This was the *Pen-t'sao kang-mu* (本草綱目) or Encyclopaedia of Herbal Medicine. It was compiled by Li Shih-chen (李時珍) and was published near the end of the sixteenth century. It took him more than a quarter of a century to collect all the works and references on herbal medicine available at the time. It gives de-

Cheng Ho came from a Muslim family and spoke Arabic well. Many South-east Asian countries had started to follow the religion of Islam by this time. This was perhaps one of the main reasons why he was chosen. His voyages led him to nearly all the countries of South-east Asia, including Annam, Cambodia, Malacca, Siam, Java, Sumatra, Borneo, Cochin, Ceylon and even Bengal in India, Arabia, Somalia in East Africa and Ormuz on the Persian Gulf. We are not sure why Yung-lo sent Cheng Ho on these costly voyages. Perhaps he sent him to hunt down his nephew who was rumoured to be hiding in South-east Asia and waiting for a chance to return. This was not a needless worry as large Chinese communities had already settled in many cities in South-east Asia. Perhaps he wanted to extend Chinese influence to that area. Whatever the reasons, there was no doubt that Ming China was a major sea-power. Cheng Ho could assemble as many as two hundred vessels which carried 30 000 men on one expedition. His voyages also proved that Chinese navigational science was already quite advanced. This was all the more remarkable if we remember that Cheng Ho's expeditions took place eighty years before the Europeans had opened up a sea route to the East.

The voyages were discontinued shortly after Yung-lo's death. Although they helped to extend Chinese influence, and also brought back strange gifts of spices, precious stones and rare animals like ostriches and giraffes, the expeditions were far too costly. Yung-lo's less ambitious successors, therefore, did not continue with this policy. After Yung-lo's death, the Ming dynasty survived for two more centuries but the peak of its power was past. Signs of decline appeared; some had their beginnings even in Yung-lo's reign. The very fact that Cheng Ho, the eunuch, was given such an important position showed that eunuchs could have an important influence. They were quarrelsome, small-minded men at court and because they were so close to the emperor they gained an influence they did not deserve. Indeed the eunuchs at one stage became so powerful that they kept an army of private guards in the royal palace. This naturally weakened the effectiveness of the government because the eunuchs were against any official who dared to criticise them. Meanwhile the officials were divided into rival groups who fought with each other for power. The treasury was exhausted. Although naval expeditions were discontinued, enormous sums of money were spent on fighting Japanese pirates. They were called *wo-k'ou* (倭寇) or *wako* in Japanese, and operated mainly in the coastal provinces. Later, Chinese pirates joined them. They generally used off-shore islands as bases from where they raided the mainland, looting and killing. Their strike-and-run tactics made it difficult to locate and destroy them. The wars fought with Japan in Korea were also very costly (see Chapter 11). The many campaigns against the Mongols and the new threat, the Manchus, made heavy demands on the treasury.

The weakness of the government encouraged rebel forces to rise in revolt. Uprisings by peasants were common in China. Even Hung-wu himself had once been a rebel leader. In 1628, when famine conditions hit the north-western province of Shensi (陝西) a group of rebels under the leadership of Li Tzu-ch'eng (李自成) rose to power. In 1644 they attacked Peking. As the rebels poured into the capital, the palace guards either fled or were killed. To avoid capture, the Ming emperor hanged himself from a plum tree on the hill overlooking the palace.

Things To Do

1 Answer in a short paragraph: Who were the border peoples troubling the Sung empire before the coming of the Mongols? How did the Sung deal with them?

2 Describe briefly the achievements of Genghis Khan and Kublai Khan.

3 Using a sentence for each, write what you consider to be the three most important points about Yüan rule.

4 Write a short story about Chu Yüan-chang before he became emperor.

5 Both Hung-wu and Yung-lo encouraged cultural activities. Do you know why? Give your answer in a short paragraph.

6 Build a model of one of Cheng Ho's ships and arrange a class competition.

7 What were the main causes of Ming decline? Give your answer in a short paragraph.

8 Write short notes on five of the following:

Temüjin	Mongol cavalry
Kublai Khan	Ch'üan-chou
Cambaluc	Yung-lo
Cheng Ho	Matteo Ricci

A Chinese porcelain sculpture of a Buddhist monk

A Chinese emperor's throne of the Ch'ing Dynasty

A Chinese dish of the Ming Period

A tapestry hanging of the Ming Period

A Ming painting of a basket of flowers

A Japanese samurai

2
Japan – to the Rise of the Tokugawas

Emperor Go-Daigo

When Yoritomo, the warrior leader we read about in Book Two, died in 1199, power fell into the hands of a family called the Hojo. They ruled the country through the shoguns and the emperor, the latter being no more than a puppet ruler. The Hojo government inherited the strong military organisation that Yoritomo had set up in Kamakura. In time, Kamakura became also a place of luxury and refinement. Tea drinking was introduced from China, and the Japanese began to make fine porcelain for the tea ceremony. This ceremony was associated with Zen Buddhism.

During this period, Japan was seriously threatened by invasion from the Mongols under their Emperor Kublai Khan. It took all the strength of the Japanese warriors to defend their country. They were helped by the elements, for a raging storm destroyed the fleets of the invading armies. Thus Japan remained the one civilised state in the Far East that had resisted the Mongols. Yet soon after the defeat of the Mongols, the shoguns' government gradually lost control over the samurai and the country began to break up.

The loyalty of the samurai towards the Hojo house weakened with the passing of time. The war with the Mongols demanded great sacrifices but brought with it no rewards. The samurai were often in debt and chose to ally themselves with influential lords who offered better prospects. These lords were the predecessors of the future *daimyo,* which literally means 'great name'.

An emperor, called Go-Daigo, took advantage of this state of confusion to rise against the Hojo shoguns. Go-Daigo became emperor in 1318 and was determined to overthrow Hojo domination. But the shogunate forced him to step down in favour of another candidate to the throne, so Go-Daigo rose up against them. This was in 1331. With the help of the great monasteries in Kyoto and other local leaders loyal to him, he held out against the shoguns' forces for some time but was eventually captured and sent into exile on the island of Oki in the Sea of Japan. Two years later, Go-Daigo escaped from his place of exile. A famous general sent by the government to fight him joined the emperor instead. He was called Ashikaga Takauji. The combined imperial forces advanced to take Kamakura itself. The last Hojo shogun, together with 800 of his closest followers, committed the ceremonial suicide of *seppuku* rather than face capture. For the Japanese, no disgrace was greater than capture and they thought it better to die by their own hands than to be tortured by their enemy.

The Mongol invasion

The Ashikaga Shoguns

The alliance between Ashikaga and Go-Daigo proved to be short-lived. No sooner was Ashikaga sure of his position than he turned against the emperor and put his own chosen candidate on the throne. Go-Daigo fled to the southern mountains and set up a rival court. The struggle went on long after the two leaders had died, and the two courts were not unified until 1392.

Ashikaga succeeded in establishing a long line of shoguns (1338–1573). He chose a district in Kyoto, known as Muromochi, as his seat of government instead of Kamakura, and so these years became known as the Muromochi Period.

During the Muromochi Period, the country seldom enjoyed peace for long. Feudal battles were common. In the fifteenth century civil strife was particularly violent and the country suffered further from a series of hardships in the form of famines and epidemics. The fates of military families changed rapidly. Many great families were uprooted only to give way to other local lords who eventually suffered the same fate themselves. The imperial house became very poor. One emperor was forced to sell his calligraphy in the streets to keep his family alive. It was almost two months after the death of another emperor before his relatives could collect enough money to give him a decent burial.

An Ashikaga shogun

In 1573 the last of the Ashikaga shoguns was driven into exile by a minor lord called Oda Nobunaga. In effect this spelled the end of the shogunate although it still survived in name until 1597 when the last shogun died.

In spite of the confusion and disasters which marked this period, the last few decades of Ashikaga rule saw the rise of many big towns. There was the town of Nara growing up around the busy temples there. There was also the port-town of Sakai which later grew into the modern city of Osaka. Japanese traders were very active in overseas trade in the whole of Asia, especially in the trade with Korea and China. Japanese pirates, the dreaded wako, attacked towns and villages on the coasts of Korea and China and this had the effect of stimulating trade rather than discouraging it.

Buddhism, especially the Zen sect, attracted many followers. So strong was the influence of Zen that it affected the work of most artists and poets of the period. Landscape gardening flourished too, and some of the best known Japanese gardens date from this period. But the most characteristic

Oda Nobunaga in a battle at Tokyo

16

form of art by far was the part-dance, part-opera, masked performance known as *no* drama. This form of art grew out of ancient court dances and popular mimes. Even today, the *no* is still performed in Japan.

Control by Military Leaders

The unsettled state of the late Ashikaga period was brought to an end by three outstanding leaders whose names have always been closely linked together. They were Nobunaga (1534–1582), Hideyoshi (1536–1598) and Tokugawa Ieyasu (1542–1616). Their share in unifying Japan is well illustrated by a popular expression: 'Nobunaga prepared the cake, Hideyoshi baked it, and Ieyasu ate it.'

Oda Nobunaga was the son of a minor daimyo and was sixteen years old when he inherited his father's lands. He began his career by expanding his own territory either by conquering or marrying his relatives into the families of his neighbours. He also made full use of the newly imported weapon, the musket, to help him win his battles. Gradually he became the most powerful daimyo in the whole country. He built himself a grand wooden palace at Azuchi on the eastern shore of the beautiful Lake Biwa in central Japan.

He dealt with the powerful Buddhist monasteries without mercy and completely broke their military power, thus ending their influence in politics which they had used in the preceding centuries. At the same time, Nobunaga was very hospitable to the Jesuit missionaries who began to visit Japan under the guidance of Francis Xavier. We shall see how missionaries came to Japan in the next section. Nobunaga granted them many audiences, although he refused to be converted to Christianity. One Jesuit priest wrote of him: 'He does not believe in the life to come, nor in anything he cannot see for himself.'

Hideyoshi was Nobunaga's best general. He had risen from the low rank of a foot-soldier by ability and hard work. While Hideyoshi was fighting in the western region in 1582, Nobunaga was murdered by

Hideyoshi

one of his generals in the capital. Hideyoshi immediately returned and killed the traitor. A fierce struggle for leadership began among the chief supporters of Nobunaga, but Hideyoshi was the strongest and he finally made peace with his chief rival, Tokugawa Ieyasu. By the end of the sixteenth century, therefore, Japan was at last unified under one man's rule.

Hideyoshi's wife

Francis Xavier

battles to fight. Hideyoshi decided to use them to increase his own power and invaded the neighbouring country of Korea. The conquest of Korea was intended to be the prelude to the conquest of China. A total of 300 000 men were sent on two campaigns to Korea in 1592 and 1597. Massive Chinese reinforcements crossed the Yalu River to aid the Koreans and forced the invaders to retreat, but they were only partly successful.

After Hideyoshi died in 1598 Japanese power in Korea diminished. Tokugawa Ieyasu, the man who had been Hideyoshi's main rival, now succeeded him. In 1603, Ieyasu formally assumed the title of shogun, which neither Nobunaga nor Hideyoshi had taken. Thus began the long reign of the Tokugawa shogunate which lasted until 1867.

Christianity in Japan

The period 1549–1614 has been called the Christian century in Japan. During this time, Christian missionaries played a very important part in bringing the West into contact with Japan. In 1543, some Portuguese merchants on their way to Macao were blown off course by a typhoon and landed in Japan. Their arrival caused considerable excitement. Their hosts took particular interest in the guns called muskets they carried with them, and this was how Nobunaga came to use them. Soon gunsmiths in Japan were making fire-arms of their own. This unexpected visit also opened a profitable trade

Hideyoshi was an ugly man and was clumsy in his movements, so he was nicknamed 'Monkey Face'. But he was such an able ruler that he won the respect of his followers. He strictly forbade commoners to wear or keep swords and maintained order by making it very difficult for anyone to move from one social class to another. He put the chaotic money system in order by issuing new coins, and introducing land and tax reforms. By these methods, Hideyoshi was able to ensure a certain measure of peace and order in the country. There remained the problem of the useful employment of the restless samurai, who had no more feudal

Portuguese merchants unloading goods at a Japanese harbour

between Macao and Japan. Not long after, Christian missionaries of the Jesuit order came with the merchants and, in 1549, the famous Francis Xavier arrived in Japan. He stayed only two years but during that time he laid a firm foundation for missionary activities. He found the prospects very promising. He wrote: '[The Japanese] are people of very good manners, good in general and not spiteful'. Soon other Jesuits followed in his footsteps. Many local daimyo, especially those in western Japan, were eager to trade with the Portuguese and therefore welcomed the missionaries. Christian converts became more and more numerous. It was estimated that in 1582 there were 150 000, in 1600 there were 300 000 and by 1615 there were 500 000.

The contact with the Portuguese brought with it many changes. Many cities grew rich from the foreign trade. New weapons meant that the Japanese had to build stronger castles to defend themselves. People benefited from new plants, such as the potato and tobacco which were introduced from America. Even Portuguese words found their way into the Japanese language.

The Closing of the Country

At first trade and missionary activities prospered side by side in Hideyoshi's reign but gradually the situation changed. Hideyoshi was afraid that the powerful lords who were friendly with the Portuguese might band together against him. At this time Spanish missionaries from the Philippines were active as well and the shogun was even more suspicious of them than of the Portuguese. In 1587 he ordered the banishment of all missionaries from Japan. Later, as this was not obeyed, he had some missionaries executed. Generally, however, he did not carry through the persecution seriously as he still found the trade very profitable.

When Ieyasu took over, he continued to let the foreigners operate in Japan but became increasingly impatient with the petty quarrels between the Portuguese and the Spaniards. He felt that he could safely get rid of the missionaries without seriously hurting the foreign trade, especially with

the arrival of English and Dutch merchants who were more anxious to trade than to preach. From 1606 Ieyasu issued order after order against Christianity. When Ieyasu died in 1616 his son continued his policy and carried out large-scale persecutions during the following year. Many missionaries and their converts faced torture and martyrdom. The shogun became even more angry with the Christians when a group of them defied his ban and, in 1638, made a last stand from a castle in Shimabara near Nagasaki. The castle was taken only with the help of the cannon fire of Dutch vessels three months later. Some 37 000 people were executed.

The Tokugawa shogunate became convinced that the missionaries and traders could not be trusted: a foreign religion might lead to foreign domination. Above all else the shogunate wanted to maintain peace and order. Gradually the country was closed to foreign trade. English merchants had already given up the Japanese trade because it was no longer profitable. The Spaniards and the Portuguese were later expelled, and the Portuguese envoys sent on a mission to re-open the trade were executed.

Two Portuguese men drawn by a Japanese artist

In 1636 the shogunate ordered that no Japanese was allowed to go abroad. Overseas Japanese were forbidden to return. Later, the construction of large ships capable of making long journeys was banned. The period of Japanese commercial expansion overseas was thus brought to a sudden end. Only a small exception was allowed. Chinese and Dutch merchants were allowed to carry on a very limited and strictly supervised trade. Dutch merchants were granted the special privilege of keeping a trading post on a small island called Deshima which was connected to the port of Nagasaki by a narrow causeway.

The Tokugawa Government

The Tokugawa shoguns made it their chief task to ensure peace and order. Gradually, building on the foundation laid by Nobunaga and Hideyoshi, the Tokugawa system of government was formed. Judging by the fact that the shogunate survived for over two and a half centuries, the system can be said to have been very successful.

The samurai were maintained as a separate and superior social class. Together with their families, they made up about five per cent of the total population. They were given the privilege of wearing their two famous swords, one long and one short, in public. In theory, they were permitted to punish there and then any commoner who did not treat them with respect. Other social classes were forbidden to marry into samurai families. A Law of the Military Houses which was later known as *Bushido* (Law of the Warrior) set down clearly the duties and virtues of a true warrior. A samurai was expected to be a scholar first and a specialist in the martial arts second. Schools were established to train warriors in such subjects as swordsmanship, fencing and judo. A samurai was taught to be loyal and obedient to his master, to be kind to the weak and to live frugally. The samurai class, once in firm control, became the chief support of the Tokugawa system of government.

The Han

The shogunate allowed the system of feudal rule to continue. It did not try to rule the country by sending out officials from the central government situated at Edo. Instead, the daimyo were allowed to rule their lands in their own way as long as they remained loyal to the Tokugawa shogunate. The daimyo were divided into three main kinds. Those related to the Tokugawa family and those who were loyal were given special lands around the capital in central Japan, and also at important points throughout the country. Other daimyo were given districts in less strategic areas. Each province that was ruled by one daimyo was called a *han*. Although the han paid no direct taxes to Edo, the daimyo were expected to present costly gifts to the shogun, to provide soldiers when asked and to carry out huge public construction projects. No marriages between daimyo families were allowed without prior permission from Edo. Fortifications were not to be built nor could existing ones be repaired. Spies were stationed in all parts of the country to forewarn the shogun of any trouble.

A man and a woman making a sword

The Sankin-Kotai System

The daimyo were further controlled by the system of *sankin-kotai*, or 'attendance by turn'. They were required to stay in Edo for varying intervals, roughly every alternate year. When they left the capital to go to their province, the family had to remain behind as hostages so that the daimyo would not make trouble. The route into the city was decided in advance and there were always ceremonial processions. These proved to be a great financial burden for the daimyo as the cost of the trip and the necessity of maintaining a permanent mansion in the capital was enormous. Well over half of the daimyo's annual income from taxes was spent on this alone. For the shogun, this was a satisfactory arrangement, as the daimyo were kept under control and their constant travelling and colourful processions necessitated the maintenance of good roads, rest-inns and other facilities. The most famous highway, called the Tokaido, was the road from Kyoto to Edo. In the capital itself, the daimyo contributed to the gay and prosperous atmosphere of the city, each competing with the other in luxury and pomp.

City Life

The long peace Japan enjoyed under the Tokugawa shoguns brought with it great prosperity in spite of the absence of foreign trade. A lot of money was spent on water control and irrigation projects. Crops such as cotton, tobacco and sugar cane were grown to meet the increasing demand. Silk farming continued to be popular as well. The quickened tempo of trade encouraged the greater use of money. People could afford to save and to make good use of their money by investing it wisely.

There grew up a class of rich merchants, especially the rice merchants of Osaka. They owned rice shops, rich warehouses, banks, fleets of vessels which sailed in the Inland Sea as well as luxurious mansions in which they lived. The merchants became in time much more important than their

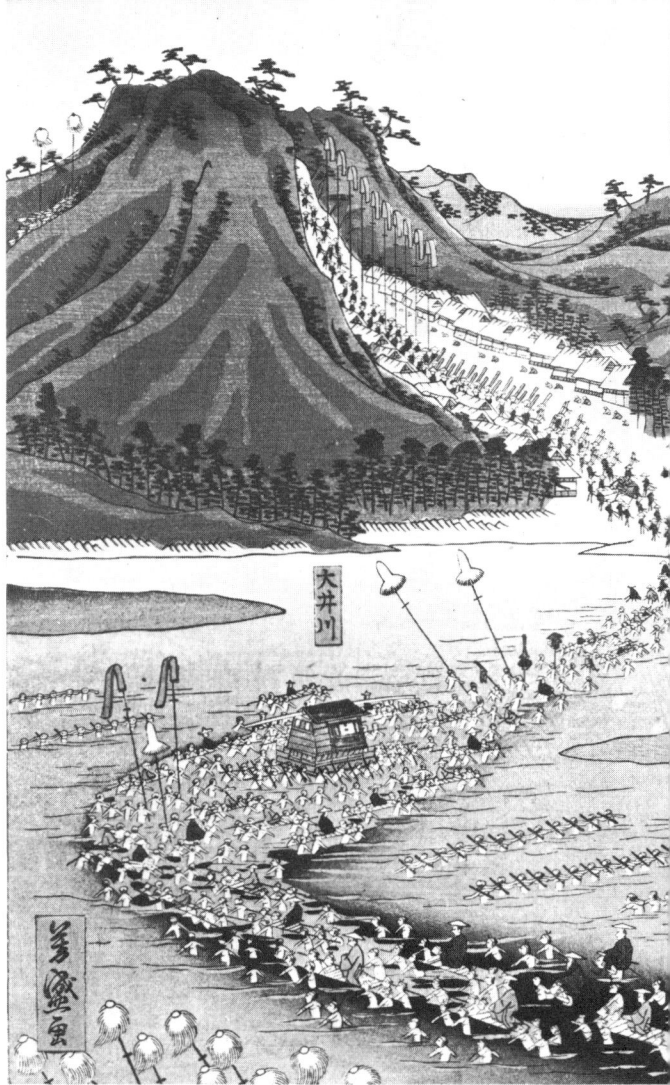

A daimyo's procession leaving the city

Osaka castle

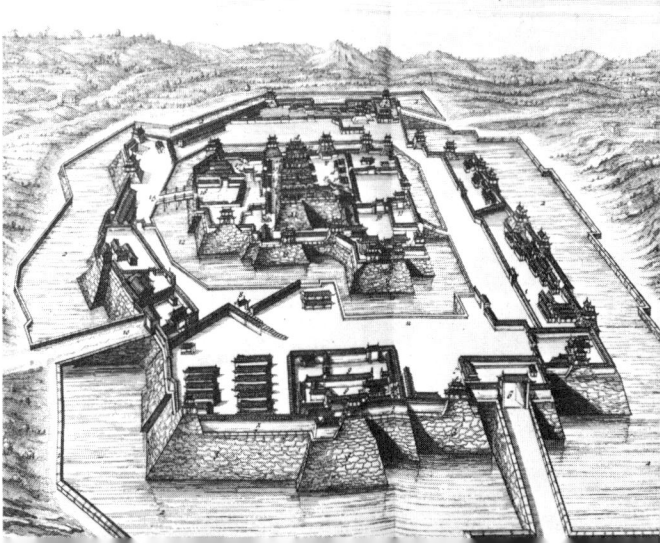

21

social position suggested. They were often creditors to poor samurai and daimyo. Some poor samurai even married into rich merchant families for the money, thereby giving their titles to them. Cities grew creating a class of townsmen known as *chonin*. Osaka in the west and Edo in the east were Japan's largest cities and throughout the eighteenth century many people were moving away from the restricted life of the farms to the cities which offered more freedom and greater opportunities for prosperity. The amusement quarters, bath houses, theatres and restaurants made life in the city seem more attractive and these places became a favourite subject matter for artists.

Although the *no* drama was still performed, its very old-fashioned and duller style was not as popular with the fun-loving townsfolk as the new form of stage performance called *kabuki*, or popular drama.

A drawing of an actor by Hokusai

A scene at the Kabuki theatre

The actors no longer wore masks. Expressions and emotions were exaggerated and humour and action were included in generous measure. In the art and literature of the period the *ukiyo*, or 'fleeting world' style, describing the richness and freedom of town life was very popular.

Ukiyo was in the beginning a Buddhist term. It was used to describe how unimportant life in the present is. In time it came to have the same meaning as 'fashionable' or 'up-to-date'. The usual heroes in the ukiyo art were such characters as 'actors, dancers, singers, story-tellers, jesters, dissolute samurai and naughty apprentices'.

The artistic sensitivity, characteristic of the Japanese, showed itself especially in the art of woodblock printing. This was much more refined than printing in the West and served as an inspiration to European artists and printers. Artists such as Hokusai were highly valued in the West.

22

A screen showing different ways of colour printing

Dutch Learning

The shoguns' policy of closing the country to foreign trade cut off the influence of the outside world, but it failed to stop the curiosity of Japanese scholars. Instead, it increased their desire to know about the outside world, and so the limited contact with the Dutch which was allowed through Nagasaki became the vital link between Japan and the rest of the world. In 1720 the shogun had to relax the ban on the import of foreign books. He even encouraged officials to take up foreign studies. This came to be known as *Rangaku,* or Dutch Learning. In 1745 the first Dutch-Japanese dictionary appeared. This was followed by many other books on scientific and technical subjects, especially medicine and military science.

Signs of Change

In outward form the Tokugawa shogunate managed to keep Japan in very much the same state in the nineteenth century as in the seventeenth century. Inwardly, many factors indicated otherwise. The declining power and status of the samurai class, the rise of the cities and the growing importance of the chonin, the learning of modern ideas, were all signs of greater changes to come.

Things To Do

1 Write a sentence about each of the following to explain their meaning:
Shogun   samurai   Zen
wako   daimyo   *no*
chonin   sankin-kotai   han
kabuki   ukiyo

2 Choose three people whom you think were most important in the period described in this chapter and write five short sentences about each one of them.

3 Explain why the Christians were successful at first but were later persecuted.

4 Explain how Japan came to be closed to foreign trade.

5 Explain briefly how the Tokugawa shoguns governed the country.

6 Compare briefly Tokugawa city life with city life of today.

7 Make a collection of pictures showing life in Tokugawa times for class exhibition. Show special points of interest by suitable labels.

8 Make a poster-exhibition showing the development of fire-arms through the centuries. Also show, if possible, actual models of various types of hand-guns.

3
Europe – Reform and Revolution

The period 1500 to 1800 in Europe was a time of great change. The boundaries between countries were not fixed by international agreement as they are now. Neighbouring countries fought to gain control of disputed areas. Countries which were divided into self-governing states, such as Germany and Italy, were constantly involved in a struggle for power amongst those states.

Look at the map below and note what Europe looked like in 1789. Since 1500 the

Europe in 1789

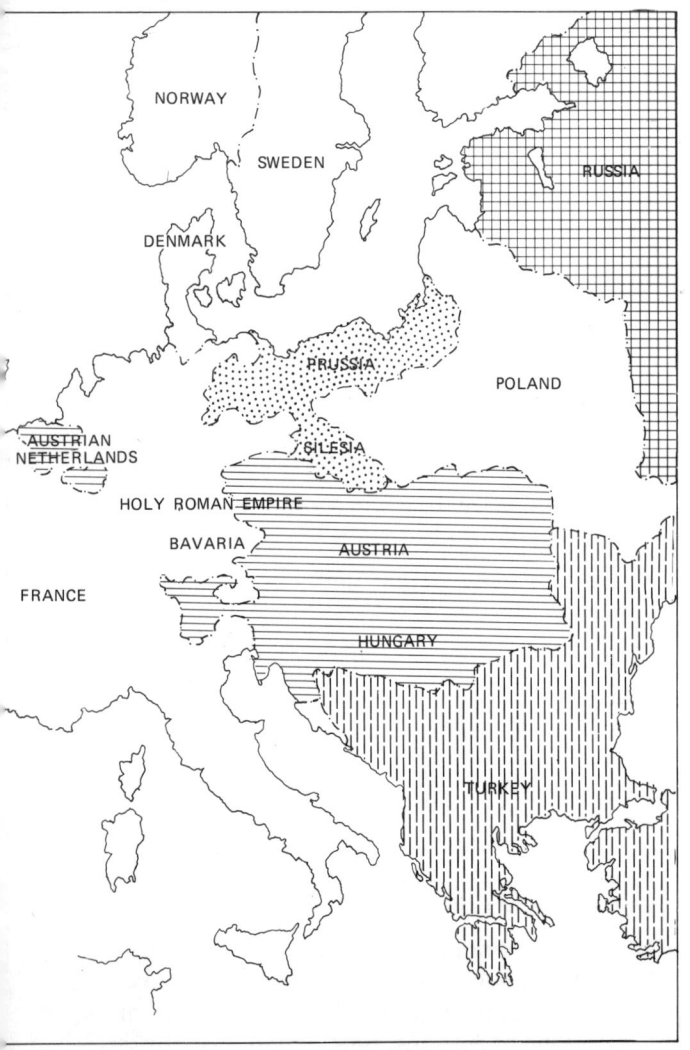

state of Prussia had increased in size and Russia had gained coastal territory along the Baltic Sea and along the north coast of the Black Sea. Perhaps the most striking development was the advance and retreat of the Ottoman or Turkish Empire. During the sixteenth century the Turks conquered large areas of Eastern Europe including Hungary and Romania, and it was not until the eighteenth century that they were driven south again into the Balkans. During these centuries the Turks were a serious threat to the nations of Europe and there were frequent wars against them.

England and Henry VIII

One of the causes for tension in Europe was that the Holy Roman Empire, once so strong, was losing its supremacy. Martin Luther's movement of protest against the Roman Catholic Church which began in 1517 had its effect in countries all over Europe. (We read about the Reformation in Book Two). Holland began a long struggle for religious freedom and independence from Catholic Spain, which ruled her until she became a Protestant Republic. In England the change from Catholicism to Protestantism was achieved in a dramatic way. Henry VIII, who was then king, wanted to divorce his wife Catherine of Aragon to marry the beautiful Anne Boleyn. Catherine had not given Henry a son and he wanted to re-marry so that male children would be born to continue his family. But the Catholic church did not believe in divorce and the Pope refused to declare that the first marriage had been illegal as Henry wanted. Henry found it intolerable that he should have to obey the Pope. Luther's reformation in Germany had created an atmosphere which made it possible for England to break from the church of Rome. In a glorious battle known as the Field of the Cloth of Gold, he defeated

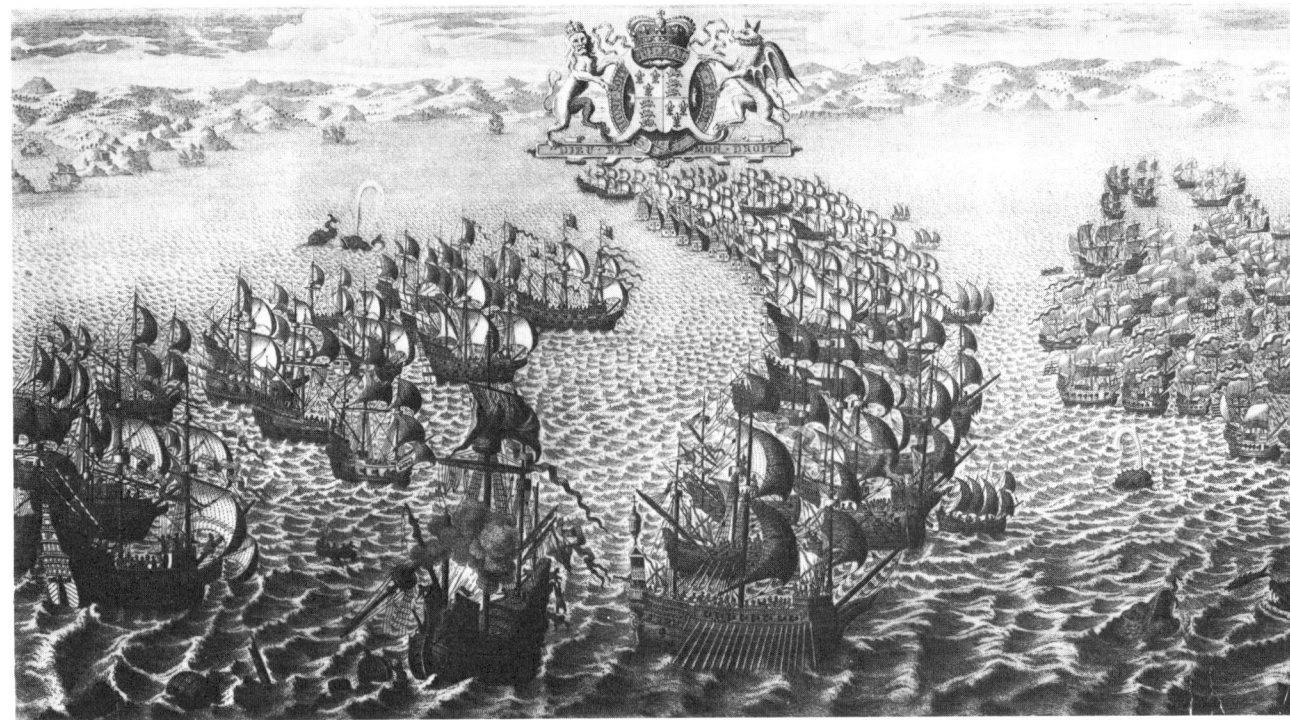

The Spanish Armada

the Emperor's forces and declared himself head of the newly-established Church of England. The Bible was translated into English and services began to be held in English rather than Latin.

Elizabeth I

Henry married Anne Boleyn as he had wanted. He was famous for the number of wives he had — six altogether. See if you can find out who his other wives were. Henry did not have a son by Anne Boleyn, but a daughter who became a great queen. This was Elizabeth I who ruled for forty-five years. Under Elizabeth, Protestantism was firmly established and England had a period of peace and prosperity. One of Elizabeth's greatest achievements was to establish Britain's supremacy on the seas. For many years English ships had been attacking Spanish treasure ships which were bringing back gold from Spanish South America. Relations between England and Spain were very strained and in 1588 the king of Spain sent an armed force of ships, an Armada, to invade England. The English fleet attacked them as they sailed up the Channel and again when they anchored off the French coast. The English were determined to win. They brought light cannons on board their ships and fired at the Spaniards who were not so well armed. Then the English sent ships which had been set on fire among them. The wind blew them directly to the Spanish ships who fled in terror; they then ran into terrible storms which wrecked many of their ships on the English coast. The remaining ships did not attack England, but sailed all the way round the north of Scotland and Ireland, where more ships were wrecked; the survivors returned to Spain. The English rejoiced that they had defeated the Spanish Armada.

The Elizabethan age has been called The Golden Age. England achieved power on the seas. Explorers like Drake and Raleigh brought the country honour and riches by their achievements. Drake sailed round the world and Raleigh founded the state of Virginia in America. This state was named after Elizabeth who was also called the Virgin Queen because she never married. It

25

was a Golden Age for music and literature too. England's most famous poet and playwright, William Shakespeare, began to write during Elizabeth's reign. His plays are colourful and exciting stories of both heroes and ordinary people. They are full of lively humour, often written in beautiful poetry, and frequently make very wise and perceptive comments on the problems and tragedies of human life.

King and Parliament

Elizabeth was the last monarch of the Tudor family. As she had no children, her distant cousin, James Stuart, the king of Scotland, became king of England too. When James came to the throne in 1603, Parliament, which was made up of advisers to the king and representatives of the people, was very strong. The members had the power to persuade the king to adopt their policies and they could refuse to allow him to raise money for foreign wars. This meant that, whether James liked it or not, the country was governed by king and Parliament together. This was why a group of Catholic Jesuits who disliked James's treatment of them decided to try and blow up the Houses of Parliament when the King was attending.

Guy Fawkes and other conspirators

In the days of the Tudor monarchs, government could be overthrown by killing the king—now both King and Parliament had to be destroyed.

However, the attempt failed because one of the conspirators sent a message to warn one of his friends not to go to Parliament that day. This friend told the King's advisers and they organised a search of the cellars under the Houses of Parliament. There they found many barrels of gunpowder and a conspirator called Guy Fawkes. Guy Fawkes confessed and the other conspirators were arrested. Since then, children in England have made bonfires and set off fireworks on 5 November, Guy Fawkes Day.

'Remember, remember
The Fifth of November!
Gunpowder, treason and plot.
I see no reason
Why gunpowder treason
Should ever be forgot!'

The Civil War

Unsuccessful wars with France during James I's reign made the King even more unpopular and there were continual quarrels between King and Parliament. The conflict came to a head in the reign of James's son Charles I who came to the throne in 1625. For eleven years, Charles tried to rule without Parliament and set himself up as an absolute monarch. This meant he was responsible to no one. But his actions only made the opposition of the parliamentarians more determined. Finally they rose up against him and there was a bitter civil war fought between the royalist supporters of the King and the supporters of Parliament, who called themselves Roundheads because they cut their hair short and wore round helmets. After four years, the Roundheads won the war. They tried the King, found him guilty of leading the country into terrible struggles, and executed him in 1649. The kings of Europe were shocked, and many people thought it wrong to kill the King because they believed he was chosen by God to rule the country.

The leader of the Roundheads was a man named Oliver Cromwell, and he took control

The execution of Charles I

after the King's death. He called himself the Lord Protector and the country became known as a Commonwealth. Oliver Cromwell belonged to a very strict group of Christians called Puritans who believed that people should lead as simple and correct lives as possible. Dancing, plays and other amusements were forbidden and both men and women had to wear simple dark clothes and there were heavy fines for drunkenness and any other misbehaviour. Cromwell ruled until he died in 1658. After his death there was no strong ruler to take his place.

The Restoration

Charles's children all fled abroad to France.

They expected that a day would come when they would be called back to their rightful heritage, and in 1660 the Parliament of the Commonwealth decided to restore the monarchy. Charles II was proclaimed king and he rode into London with much ceremony and rejoicing. The years of his reign were happy ones, and there was a release from the hardships of Cromwell's rule. Charles himself loved fine clothes, pleasures and the theatre, and so encouraged others with these tastes. New plays were written and fine buildings were put up. On the whole, Charles was a popular king, who ruled with Parliament. But his brother James II who succeeded the childless Charles was not liked. He made no secret of the fact that he

A Civil War battle

Charles II dancing at court

William in Parliament

German prince, George, who ruled a small state in North Germany called Hanover. George came to England to be crowned in 1714. George spoke hardly any English and left the government of the country to his ministers in Parliament. In this way, Parliament gained more and more power and the King less and less. As the importance of Parliament grew, the differences between the two parties in the House of Commons became more marked. The Tory Party believed in traditionalism and strongly supported the King, whereas the Whig Party welcomed changes.

The three kings who succeeded the first George were also called George and so the period became known as the Georgian era.

France under Louis XIV

While England was undergoing struggles between the king and the people, France was being ruled by a strong king called Louis XIV who reigned from 1643–1715. Louis was an absolute monarch and it is partly because the English kings envied his power that they tried to copy him and so entered into conflict with Parliament. Louis' court was the most colourful and rich in the whole of Europe. His palace at Versailles, near Paris, with its hall of mirrors, its terraces, fountains, parks and wonderful furniture was admired by the world. Louis himself was admired and is sometimes called the Sun King. He wore tall powdered wigs, silk

was a Catholic and tried to introduce laws to help Catholics against the wishes of Parliament. He only reigned for three years before he was forced to flee the country in 1688.

The Glorious Revolution

In 1688 William of Orange and his wife Mary, who was James's daughter, came from Holland to be crowned as joint king and queen. Mary was the next in line of succession (excluding James II's family), but her husband refused to allow her to be crowned unless he was given equal privileges. With the coronation came new laws giving increased power to Parliament so that, ever since, kings and queens of England have had to rule with the advice and consent of Parliament. This is called 'constitutional monarchy'. William and Mary were so popular that people called this 'The Glorious Revolution' because it was a revolution without fighting and bloodshed.

The Georgians

William and Mary were succeeded by Mary's sister, Anne, who was married to a Danish prince. Unfortunately all of her many children died young and the next heir was a

Louis XIV and his family

French revolutionaries prepare to storm the Bastille

and lace shirts, embroidered waistcoats and high heeled red shoes which were decorated with rosettes. Music, art and literature flourished in France at this time, and France seemed to be rich and prosperous. But Louis and his courtiers could only live in such luxury because the poor were very highly taxed. This made him very unpopular among the working people. So also did the disastrous and expensive wars in which Louis involved the country. By the time he died the country was exhausted. Louis was succeeded by weak kings who did nothing to put the country in better shape.

The French Revolution

By 1787 the French monarchy found itself bankrupt. The King, Louis XVI, and his Austrian wife Marie Antoinette, were living more extravagantly than they could afford and were setting an example of costly living to the nobles at court. The tenants who lived on their lands were taxed more and more highly to provide money for the luxuries their landlords desired.

In 1789 the King summoned a gathering of nobles, clergy and commoners together to try to sort out his financial situation. This gathering was called the States General and it was like the English Parliament. Like the English, its representatives decided that they would only help the King in his financial troubles if he agreed to rule with them and become a constitutional monarch. But the King would not agree and so the representatives formed themselves into a ruling body known as the National Assembly which was determined to keep the King in order. The storming of the terrifying Bastille prison marked the beginning of the revolution and the end of absolute monarchy in France. It also marked the rise of the *bourgeoisie*, that is, the middle classes, who began to show their grievances. They demanded lower food prices, less taxation, and equal opportunities and rights for all people. The slogan of the people of France was *'Liberté, Fraternité, Egalité ou la Mort'*, which means 'Liberty, Brotherhood, Equality or Death'. Many aristocrats who had treated their tenants badly were put to death. The King himself, when he tried to flee the country, was brought back and executed. Like Charles I in England, he was tried by the people who decided that he was a traitor to the country and must die.

The Republic

So France became a Republic. All enemies of the Republic were put to death and a period of bloodshed and rioting followed. The youth of France poured into Republican armies to fight against the neighbouring countries who were afraid that revolutionary ideas would spread to them. A general called Napoléon Bonaparte led the army in successful battles all over Europe. He was a strong leader: the kind of man France needed. Gradually he climbed towards a position of supreme power and in 1804 he declared himself Emperor of France. We shall read more about Napoléon in the next chapter.

Russia

Russia did not suffer from religious conflicts as the other countries of Europe did because the Russians were members of the Orthodox Church, whose leader had been the Patriarch of Constantinople until the Turks conquered that city in 1453. After that the Russians thought of themselves as the leaders of the Orthodox Church. There were, however, differences of belief inside the Orthodox Church between the reformers and the Old Believers, who did not want any change at all.

Peter the Great

In the late seventeenth century Russia was ruled by Peter the Great. He was a huge, very energetic man who had travelled widely in Europe and wanted to westernise and modernise Russia. He forced his courtiers to wear western dress and encouraged foreign industrial and scientific advisers to come and teach the Russians the new methods of fighting and working that he had seen in other parts of Europe, particularly England. He had himself worked in a naval dockyard in England in order to learn more about ship construction. He had a new city built on the Gulf of Finland which is part of the Baltic Sea, so that Russia would have better sea communications with the rest of Europe during the summer months when the sea was not frozen. This city was called St. Petersburg, now Leningrad. He was very impressed by some of the French palaces

The summer palace at St. Petersburg

that he had seen, so he employed a French architect to design his new city. Peter and his successors ruled Russia as absolute monarchs.

Catherine the Great

At the end of the eighteenth century Russia was ruled by a woman, Catherine the Great. It is said that she had her husband murdered and had many lovers. During her reign several wars were fought against the Turks. The Russians gained land along the north coast of the Black Sea, including the Crimean Peninsula, from the Turks. Russia could now build a warm water port, but could only use it if the Turks were friendly, because the Turks controlled the two straits at the entry to the Black Sea which are called the Straits of the Bosphorus and the Dardanelles.

Things To Do

1 Make biographical notes on all of the famous people mentioned. Use encyclopaedias and other books of reference. Find out their dates of birth and death.
2 Make a family tree of the royal families in England and France. Illustrate it with drawings.
3 Read one of Shakespeare's history plays in class.
4 Make a model of an Elizabethan playhouse or an Elizabethan ship.
5 Write short notes on the difference between an absolute monarch and a constitutional monarch.
6 Explain in a short paragraph why the execution of Charles I shocked Europe.
7 Read and discuss the following poems written by famous Georgian poets:

Keats: *Ode to a Grecian Urn*
Wordsworth: *Daffodils*
Coleridge: *Kubla Khan*

8 Make a drawing of the Court of Peter the Great. Imagine that he is giving instructions about the building of a new city.

Portrait of Queen Elizabeth I

Above *The Field of the Cloth of Gold where Henry VIII declared himself head of the Church of England*

Right *London Bridge in the sixteenth century*

Left *The Hall of Mirrors at Versailles*

Bottom left *The Gardens at Versailles*

Bottom right *Catherine the Great of Russia*

Above *The Emperor
Napoléon receives
the Queen of Prussia
at his court*

Right *Napoléon leaves his
carriage for his wedding*

4
Modern Europe

Europe under Napoléon

Napoléon

Napoléon

Napoléon Bonaparte, general of the victorious French armies and one of the most successful soldiers ever, seized power in France in 1799. In 1804 he made himself emperor of France. He had already made many improvements in France after the confusions of the revolution, such as a clear new law system, called the Code Napoléon. He made an agreement with the Pope, restoring Roman Catholicism as the official religion of France, but allowing freedom of worship to people of other faiths and religions. He made sure that local government was efficient so that people could live in peace in every part of France. The people of France were so glad to have order restored, after the violence and confusion of the previous ten years, that they accepted Napoléon and his firm government. Napoléon involved France in long wars with the other countries of Europe as he extended his empire. At first he had great success and was master of nearly all western Europe for some years. But, eventually,

Britain with the other nations of Europe defeated him in 1814. Napoléon was exiled from France and sent to live on a small island off the coast of Italy called Elba.

An empire-style party

The Treaty of Vienna

When Napoléon was defeated in 1814, the leaders of the other nations had to fix the boundaries of the countries of Europe because Napoléon had conquered many of

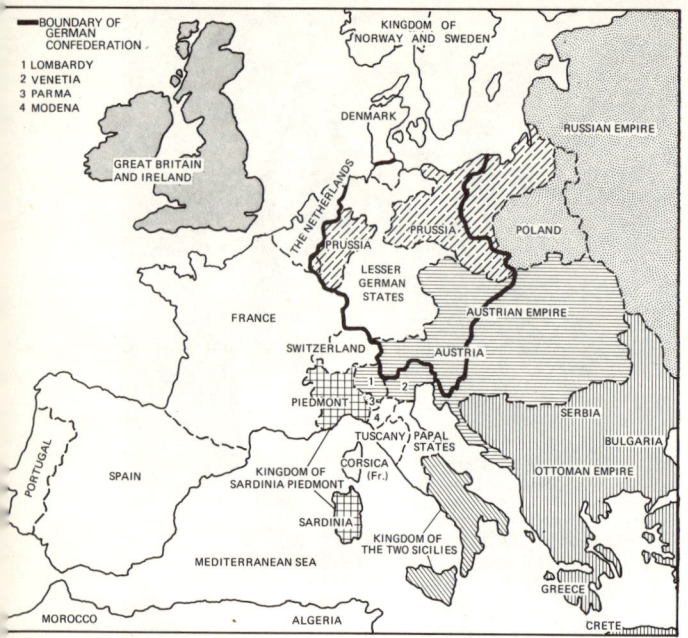

Europe in 1815

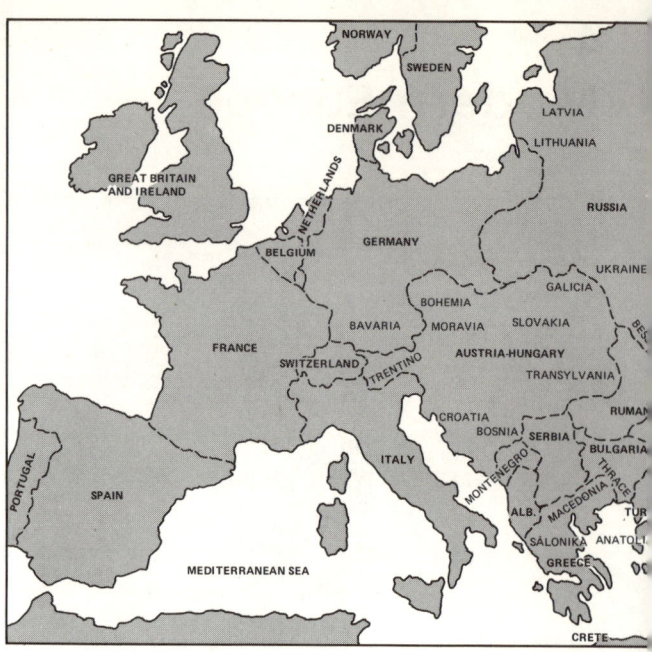

Europe in 1914

them and changed both their boundaries and their rulers. It was difficult to make a fair settlement, but the one they made at Vienna in 1814 lasted, with few changes, until the First World War in 1914. Look at the maps to see what changes were made.

While talks were being held in Vienna, Napoléon escaped from Elba and landed in the south of France. His former soldiers flocked back to join him. He soon had an army and entered Paris in triumph. The other nations prepared for war again.

Napoléon met the British army under the Duke of Wellington at Waterloo, and they fought a great battle. The British were nearly defeated but the Prussian army arrived in time to change defeat into a victory for Britain and Prussia. Napoléon was captured and sent to the island of St. Helena far away in the south Atlantic where he lived until his death in 1821.

The rulers of Europe were frightened by the violent changes which had taken place in France and by new demands for liberty in their own countries. They wanted things to be as they had been before the Revolution. For this reason they opposed all political changes in their countries.

The Battle of Waterloo

France

After Napoléon's fall, the French decided to invite the successor of their last king to come back. He was to have more limited powers. So Louis XVIII became king. He was fat and lazy, but the French people accepted him as they did not want any more changes. When he died, his brother Charles became king. Charles X wanted to go back to the old days before the Revolution, when the nobles owned most of the land and the Roman Catholic Church controlled education and censored books and newspapers. But the people would not accept this. In 1830 there was a bloodless revolution in France and Charles was forced to abdicate.

Louis Philippe

His cousin Louis Philippe became king. He lived a very ordinary life like other people and few Frenchmen liked his policies as King. At last people rose against him and made France a Republic in 1848. The first president of the Republic was Louis Napoléon, nephew of the emperor. He soon changed the new constitution and made France an empire again in 1852, with himself as Emperor Napoléon III.

Problems

France had had such violent changes in the Revolution, and so many different kinds of government, that it was very difficult for anyone to rule France successfully again. Some Frenchmen were monarchists, some were republicans, some were socialists, and some were anarchists. It was impossible to satisfy them all.

Meanwhile an industrial revolution was taking place in France. Many people were working in factories and living in crowded conditions and working very long hours. Some were very dissatisfied with their lives and supported the socialists who promised them better lives and better conditions if they overthrew the government.

Napoléon III and his wife

The French Empire

Frenchmen overseas explored and established trading posts in Africa and the Far East, and a new French empire grew up to replace the one lost by Napoléon. In North Africa, Frenchmen settled in Algeria and Tunis. Both became French colonies before 1900, and Morocco also became French before the First World War in spite of German opposition. In Indo-China French interests were developed in the countries we now call Cambodia, Laos and Vietnam, which became French protectorates. We shall read more about this in Chapter 9. The French built roads, established schools, taught the French language and ruled their colonies just as if they were a part of France.

Germany

For centuries Germany had been made up of many small independent states. Many of the large towns in these states had famous universities and, among the students and professors of the universities, ideas of 'nationalism' and 'liberalism' developed. The students and professors wanted Germany to be a single united nation and they wanted better government. They especially wanted an elected government which would allow them more freedom to write and say what they wanted without fear of being arrested by the police and put in prison. In 1848 there was a meeting in Frankfurt of representatives from all the German states. They tried to write a constitution for a new Germany, but there were many quarrels and arguments. They could not agree whether or not to include Austria and the Austrian empire. The meeting ended in confusion.

Communism

In 1848 Karl Marx and Friedrich Engels produced a book called the *Communist Manifesto,* in which they criticised the industrial societies of Europe and declared that a struggle was taking place between the rich and the poor. They said that the poor working class people would defeat the rich middle classes; they would set up working class societies throughout the world where everyone would have work and receive all that they needed for their daily life. Their ideas soon became very popular all over Europe and an International Working Men's Association was set up and first met in London in 1864.

Prussia

Prussia was one of the biggest of the thirty-nine German states, and she had a fine army and ambitious leaders. They wanted Prussia to dominate the German states. However, there was another German speaking state, Austria, which was the head of a big empire in which there were many non-German peoples. Austria and Prussia were rivals for the leadership of the German states, but by the end of the nineteenth century it was Prussia which had won.

Bismarck

In the second half of the nineteenth century, the king of Prussia had a very able minister called Bismarck. He involved Prussia in three brief, successful wars against Denmark, then Austria, and finally France. The swift victories over Austria and France showed the power of the Prussian army and made it possible to create a new German Empire in

Bismarck discusses Prussian affairs

1871, with the king of Prussia as emperor and Bismarck as chancellor. Only Austria was left out. For the next twenty years, Bismarck, a brilliant diplomat, prevented other states from uniting against the new German empire. This gave it time to grow to strength and unity.

The Austrian Empire

Austria was a German state, but the Austrian Empire also included Croats, Czechs, Hungarians, Poles, Ruthenians and Slovaks, ruled by the German-speaking government in Vienna. The Emperor's chief minister was Prince Metternich. He understood how difficult it was to rule such a varied collection of peoples under one government. His policy was to keep things as they were. He feared that change might lead to a revolution and the break-up of the Austrian Empire. While Metternich remained chancellor all demands for change were refused and all revolts severely crushed.

The Austrians in Italy

The Austrian Empire included parts of northern Italy, and Austria had great influence in Italian affairs. In 1820 there were revolts in the Italian kingdoms of Piedmont and Naples and the rulers of these states asked the Austrian government to send soldiers to help them suppress the revolts. So Austrian soldiers went to Piedmont and Naples and restored the kings to full power. In 1830 there were more revolts in Italy, this time in Parma, Modena and the Papal States. Again Austrian soldiers went to put down the rebellions. Metternich was very anxious to help the rulers of these states because he was frightened that revolution might spread to the Austrian Empire.

Many Italians, like the Germans, wanted to unite their country as one nation under one government and they were encouraged by a man called Mazzini who started a nationalist movement called 'Young Italy'. He tried to overthrow the government of Piedmont in 1830 but failed, and had to go into exile.

The Unification of Italy

During the 1850s the small northern state of Piedmont was well governed by King Victor Emmanuel II and his Prime Minister, Cavour. They were determined to drive the Austrians out of the provinces of Lombardy and Venetia. In 1859, Napoléon III of France helped Piedmont to drive the Austrians out of Lombardy. Several months later other small states in northern Italy voted to join with Piedmont under one government. In the south, Garibaldi, an adventurous leader from Piedmont, took a thousand men to Sicily, where he encouraged the people to rise against the King of Naples. Soon all southern Italy was united under Garibaldi and he handed control over to Victor Emmanuel, so that Italy could be united under one king and declared a state in 1860. Venice became part of Italy seven years later when the Prussians defeated the Austrians.

The 1848 Revolutions

In the year 1848 there were violent revolutions in almost every capital in Europe. Most of the educated people wanted a more democratic government in which they could take part. They also wanted better laws and more freedom of speech and of the press. In some countries people were trying to throw off foreign rule. In Vienna, the capital of the Austrian Empire, the Emperor and Metternich both had to leave the city while the leaders of the revolution tried to form a new government. However, there was so much argument that finally the Emperor returned to the throne. This Emperor was named Franz Josef and he ruled until 1916. During this time his wife was shot by a revolutionary, his son committed suicide, and his nephew (heir to the throne) was assassinated. In 1848 he faced revolutions not only in Vienna, but also in Prague and in Budapest. In Budapest a revolutionary leader called Kossuth set up a separate government for Hungary and it was more than a year before Austria could defeat them. In Prague the Austrian soldiers restored order more quickly. The people of Hungary and what is now called Czechoslovakia wanted to be nations in their own right, not to be ruled by the Austrians. The Austrians replied by suppressing firmly all nationalist or liberal ideas.

Hungary

However, in 1867 Hungary was allowed equal status with Austria and the empire was re-named the Dual Monarchy of Austria-Hungary. The Emperor now had a new title 'King of Hungary' as well as still being the

Garibaldi and his men fighting

Emperor of Austria. Hungary was allowed to have a separate Parliament and people were allowed to use Hungarian as their official language. This pleased the Hungarians, but it did not please the other subject peoples living in Austria-Hungary, such as the Slavs and the Croats. The Slavs were particularly jealous and longed to be part of a separate Slav state.

The 'Eastern Question'

The Turkish or Ottoman Empire had been the major power in the Middle East for centuries. This empire was now breaking up, and the rulers of Europe were watching each other carefully in case one of them tried to grasp Turkey's power. The 'question' was what was going to happen to the Empire when it had broken up. This 'Eastern Question' became serious in the nineteenth century because of the development of nationalism in the Balkan States, which were part of the Turkish Empire. Greece was the first of these states to achieve full independence. The Greeks fought for independence from 1821 to 1830 and were helped by Britain, France and Russia. These great powers all wanted the Greeks to be free from Turkish rule. After this the other Balkan states also wanted to be free and the great powers started to compete with each other for parts of the Turkish Empire. Turkey was called 'the sick man of Europe' because its Empire was breaking up. The Tsar of Russia discussed the matter with the British ambassador, but the British ambassador was worried that the Tsar would simply take over the control of the Balkans from the Turks. When the Russians invaded the Balkan States of Moldavia and Wallachia (modern Rumania) the British prepared to go to war.

The Crimean War

The war of 1854–56 was fought in the Crimean Peninsula which is in south Russia. The Russians had a naval base there called Sevastopol. The British and French armies went to the Crimea, attacked Sevastopol and captured it after nearly two years of fighting. In the peace treaty that was signed afterwards in Paris, the Russians had to promise not to use Sevastopol or the Black Sea for naval ships, but they did not keep this promise very long. Moldavia and

The Crimean War

A Russian serf and a landowner

Wallachia were given the right to govern themselves, although they were still part of the Turkish Empire.

The Crimean War was the first war to be photographed, as photography had just been invented. People could see for the first time what wars were really like. The war was also reported for the English newspaper, *The Times,* and people read about the fighting and about the bad state of the hospitals.

Balkan Problems

In the 1870s other Balkan nations rebelled against the Turks, but they did not all gain their independence. Austria, Britain and France were frightened that if the Turks lost control of the whole Balkans, the Russians would dominate instead. So it was not until 1912 that the Turks were driven out of the Balkan Peninsula, and even then they kept the city of Constantinople and the land around it. The problems of the Balkans, which the European rulers could not agree to settle, were to result in the First World War, which started in Serbia in 1914.

Russia

Alexander I to Alexander II

During the Napoleonic Wars, Russia was ruled by Alexander I, who wanted to improve the government of Russia and the condition of the people, but achieved very little constructive reform.

Alexander's son, Nicholas, succeeded him in 1825. Nicholas I was determined to rule his country firmly, using strict censorship and the secret police force. There were many peasant rebellions, but nothing was done to improve the conditions of life for the peasant farmers, many of whom were serfs. Serfs belonged to their masters, the landlords.

Nicholas I died during the Crimean War in 1855 and left his son Alexander II to make peace with Britain, France and Piedmont in 1856. He began certain reforms as soon as he became Tsar. He relaxed censorship and gave students more freedom. Alexander set up many committees to discuss the emancipation of the serfs (slaves). In 1861 the serfs were made free but they had to pay for the land that they were granted by the landlords, sometimes over a period of many years. Alexander also improved local government in Russia by setting up local councils called *zemstvos.*

Cultural Developments

During the nineteenth century there were many great authors in Russia who criticised government and society for their injustice. Some of them were imprisoned because of their writing, and one of them, Dostoyevsky, was nearly executed. Probably the greatest of them was Tolstoy, who wrote a novel about the Napoleonic Wars called *War and Peace.* Tolstoy was an aristocrat but he sympathised with the sufferings of the common people.

Some of the intellectuals were more violent in their intentions and even planned to kill the Tsar. They made several attempts to assassinate Alexander but did not succeed until 1881, when they threw a bomb at him while he was examining one of his servants who had himself been injured by another one.

Alexander III

Alexander was horrified by the death of his father and became convinced that only firm government would maintain order in Russia. He gave the nobles more power and increased censorship of the press and control over student activities. The Jews were persecuted in Russia because their way of life and beliefs were different from those of other Russians. It was difficult for them to get education and impossible to get jobs in the professions such as medicine or law. From time to time the people were encouraged to attack and kill the Jews. Many Jews tried to escape from Russia and some went back to Palestine, the home of their ancestors.

Alexander III's reign was a time of great industrial development. One of the most important Russian achievements was the building of the Trans-Siberian Railway linking western Russia with the Pacific coast at Vladivostok and making it possible to develop Siberia. This development led to a

Nicholas II inspecting the guard

desire to take over parts of Manchuria from the weak Manchu rulers in China, and to rivalry with the growing power of Japan.

In spite of much repression, opposition to the Tsar's government continued to grow, led by the Marxists and a young man who took the pseudonym, Nicolai Lenin. Lenin's brother had been executed for plotting to kill Alexander III. Lenin himself studied to be a lawyer but he also read many books on socialism and followed closely the ideas of Karl Marx. He founded a newspaper which was circulated illegally in Russia, telling people that the working class should rise up and overthrow the government and set up a society of its own.

The last tsar of Russia was Nicholas II, who wished to rule well but did not have the ability to do so. He was faced with enormous political, social and economic problems. These led to a revolution sparked off by the sufferings of the people during the First World War.

Britain

During the nineteenth century the United Kingdom (then including the whole of Ireland as well as England, Scotland and Wales) was a constitutional monarchy. For most of the century Britain was under the influence of Queen Victoria, who reigned from 1837 to 1901. When she became queen at the age of eighteen she was determined to do her best to rule well:

> 'Since it has pleased Providence to place me in this station, I shall do my utmost to fulfil my duty towards my country; I am very young, and perhaps in many, though not in all things, inexperienced, but I am sure, that very few have more real good will and more real desire to do what is fit and right than I have.'

Victoria married her cousin Albert and was very attached to him. He was a hard-working man and he studied problems in great detail. Albert advised the Queen on all matters and she relied on him. When he died in 1861, she was broken-hearted and took little part in public life for the rest of her long reign. Nevertheless she had made the British

Queen Victoria at her first parliament

monarchy widely respected and loved, and perhaps this is why it has continued even into the twentieth century when so many monarchies in other countries have been overthrown.

Parliament

As a constitutional monarch the queen ruled with the advice and consent of her Parliament. In fact, by the nineteenth century, Parliament ruled and the queen nearly always gave her consent to whatever laws or policies Parliament wished to make. Parliament consisted of the House of Lords and the House of Commons. The Lords were members of the aristocracy who had the right to attend Parliament. The bishops of the Church of England also attended the House of Lords. The House of Commons consisted of men elected by the people of England at general elections held every few years. At the beginning of the nineteenth century the poorer people could not vote because they did not own their houses or property, but, during the century, Parliament changed the voting qualifications several times to include more people. By doing this Parliament prevented Britain from having a revolution at a time when nearly every other nation in Europe had at least one. Today all men and women over eighteen can vote in Britain.

Prime Ministers

The queen had the right to choose one man from either of the Houses of Parliament to be her Prime Minister. She usually chose the leader of the biggest political group or party in Parliament. The Prime Minister chose a group of men to form his council, called the Cabinet. The Cabinet made all the decisions on government matters unless the members of the Houses of Parliament disagreed with their policies and voted against them, or until their term of office was over. Then there would be a general election. Two of Queen Victoria's greatest Prime Ministers were William Gladstone and Benjamin Disraeli. Gladstone particularly wanted to deal with some of the problems of English society, while Disraeli wanted to make England a great and respected country abroad.

Social Reforms

A great social reformer, Lord Shaftesbury, spent his life trying to get Parliament to pass laws to protect women and children and prevent them from working long hours in factories. He was very much concerned with helping young chimney sweeps—boys who were sent up the chimneys to clean them. This was difficult and dangerous work and some boys actually died in their work. Lord Shaftesbury also tried to stop the employment of children in the mines. Gradually laws were passed and by the end of the century children were no longer working in such places.

Another man who cared very much for children was Dr Barnardo. He started a home for poor children without families. He used to walk the streets of London looking for homeless children. Barnardo Homes were set up in many cities of England.

Things To Do

1 Make a list of the people mentioned in this chapter. Look up their dates of birth and death in an encyclopaedia or biographical dictionary.

2 Write a short paragraph about six of the people from the list made in question 1.

3 Make your own time chart of the nineteenth century in Europe.

4 Draw an illustrated map of Europe in the nineteenth century showing revolutions and uprisings. Put in the capital cities but not the boundaries.

5 Ask your teacher to read you one of Tolstoy's short stories.

Children at work in a coal mine

5
Europe – New Ways of Life

Newton

Scientific Development

The modern world is based on the discoveries and developments of scientists and inventors of the past three centuries. At first it was the English and French who led the way. In 1660 a society was formed in England to encourage scientists in all fields. Its full title was 'The Royal Society of London for Improving Natural Knowledge' and charter was granted by Charles II. All members decided to take no theory on trust which meant that there were continual debates and experiments to prove a new theory. One of the founder members of the Royal Society, and one of the greatest, was Isaac Newton. He was a mathematician and astronomer and his great contribution to science and knowledge was his discovery of the laws of motion and gravitation; Newton noticed three things:

1 that objects or people move in straight lines unless other forces cause them to change direction;
2 that change of motion, or direction, is proportional to the strength of the force exerted on the body;
3 that to every action there is always an equal opposite reaction.

He formulated a universal law of gravitation which was based on these observations. He was using the scientific method set down by the French mathematician and philosopher, Descartes, who thought that all ideas should be doubted until they could be proved to be true.

Eighteenth-century France was a place of great progress in science and learning. A group of men led by Diderot wrote an encyclopaedia which was eventually printed in 1772, having taken twenty-six years to write. It had seventeen volumes of text and eleven of plates. The aim was to assemble all the known facts scattered about the world and to explain all things that men might want to know about. The encyclopaedia was not sold in France until after the Revolution. It had been banned by the King because he thought spreading knowledge would establish a spirit of revolt and independence and so would lessen royal authority.

A page from the French Encyclopaedia

The French writers admired the habit of free discussion in England as they were not used to such tolerance. But in England during the nineteenth century a new theory was formed which shattered even the most tolerant people. This arose out of the conflict between science and religion in Charles Darwin's theory of evolution. Darwin was a biologist who spent many years studying plants and animals, and for five years he travelled by ship round the world visiting many places including the Galapagos Islands, west of South America, where he found very unusual plants and animals including the giant tortoise. He wrote a book called *The Origin of Species* about the evolution of plants and animals by natural selection. Some Christians thought that this contradicted the belief of the creation of the world by God as written in the Book of Genesis, although Darwin himself believed in God and had no wish to destroy Christian belief. Many people at that time wanted to examine the Bible more carefully and to study how it came to be written.

Arkwright's spinning frame

Industrial Development

Discoveries in the world of science had an important effect on industry. New machines were invented which could speed up production and replace some of the more mechanical and boring work that was done by both adults and children. The new inventions meant that more goods could be produced and so more people were needed to work on the machines. Gradually people moved to the towns to look for factory work and so industrial work began to take the place of agricultural work. There were such wide-reaching changes throughout the late eighteenth and nineteenth centuries that we call this the Industrial Revolution. The changes were taking place all over Europe, but perhaps England again was leading the way, and so we will look at some of the most important people of the industrial era.

Richard Arkwright

Richard Arkwright invented the cotton spinning frame. It was worked by water power and not by hand. Many workers were angry with him because they thought that his machine would take away the jobs of the people who had previously worked by hand. He had to leave his home town of Preston in the north of England and move to Nottingham in the Midlands. Here he set up a cotton mill driven by horses. Later he set up a larger factory at Cromford, near a stream in Derbyshire, and this was driven by water power. Workers were still angry with him,

Weaving cotton

however, and they completely destroyed one of his mills. He did not give up, and used another new invention, a steam engine, to work his mill in Nottingham.

Arkwright's troubles show us the hostility of ordinary people to some modern inventions, and the difficulty of finding satisfactory power to work the new machines. Two men are largely responsible for the development of the steam engine for industrial use.

James Watt

James Watt discovered how to improve the steam engine which had already been invented for pumping water out of the ground. His steam engine was so successful that he joined with Matthew Boulton to manufacture steam engines in Soho, Birmingham. Boulton and Watt engines were bought by many companies in England and abroad, particularly for use in mines. They were also adapted to drive machinery like that in Richard Arkwright's cotton mill.

George Stephenson

George Stephenson invented his first locomotive (moving steam engine) for the coal mine where he worked as an engineer. His ideas were based on James Watt's steam engine. He helped to construct the first railway between Stockton and Darlington which opened in 1825. Stephenson's new locomotive, called 'The Rocket', won a competition to provide an engine for the new railway and could travel at 40 mph. Railways were soon built to link together all the important cities in England as well as cities throughout Europe. It was a tremendous change. For example, after Napoléon Bonaparte's defeat in Russia, he travelled back to Paris on horse and foot in three hundred and twelve hours. Now, suddenly, the same journey was reduced to forty-eight hours!

Railways also made the transporting of goods very much easier and faster. Manufacturers were able to send their products much further and much quicker, and this helped trade to develop both in England and abroad.

The steam ship was also a development

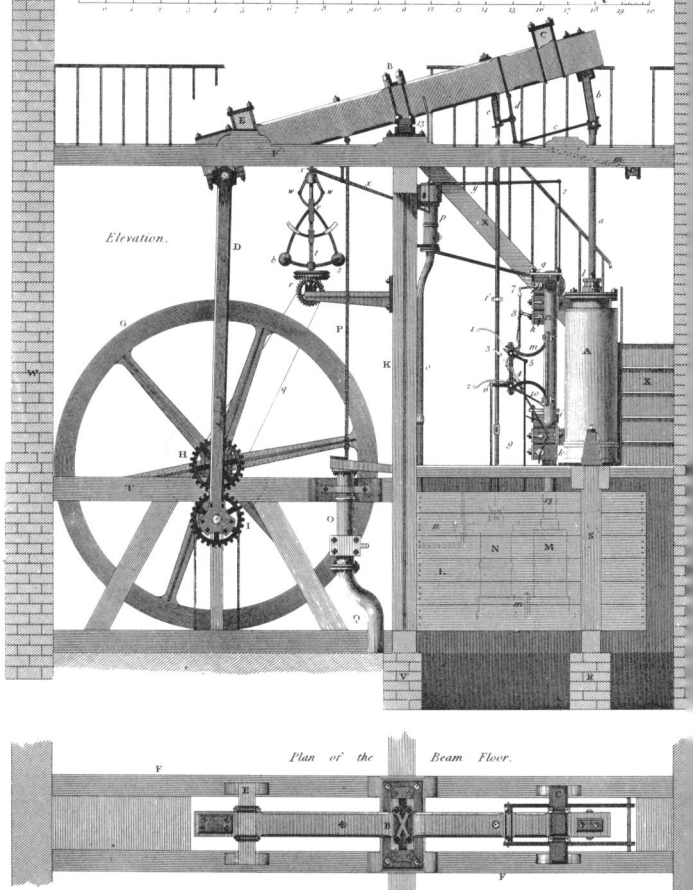

Watt's steam engine

of Watt's engine, and it too had a noticeable effect on trade. The first steam ship to sail on the sea was the *Phoenix* which went from New York to Philadelphia in 1818. As these ships had more power than the old sailing ships they could be built larger and heavier. Ships began to be built of steel and could carry much bigger cargoes.

Stephenson's engine, the Rocket

Isambard Kingdom Brunel

One of the most remarkable industrialists of the nineteenth century was Isambard Kingdom Brunel. His father had escaped from France during the Revolution and was an engineer. Young Brunel helped his father with the construction of a tunnel under the River Thames in London, and himself later built many tunnels, bridges and viaducts. He also built a very large steamship called *The Great Eastern* and he was responsible for the Great Western Railway. He was very imaginative and inventive and achieved many successes.

Housing conditions

Urbanisation

The development of factories took place in the towns of many countries in Europe, particularly in those towns near coalfields and iron ore supplies. Once steam engines had been invented, factories could be built anywhere convenient to the builder. Many people came from the country to the towns in search of work and they needed places to live. Houses were built very quickly for them and these houses were sometimes badly built and soon became overcrowded and unhealthy. There were hardly any public services, and rubbish was just left to rot in the streets. Large ugly towns grew up full of dirty slums and factories where people worked for very long hours. It was not until the twentieth century that people began to be more conscious of their environment and to replan these cities and to make them into pleasant places to live in.

Population

One of the remarkable facts about Europe in the eighteenth and nineteenth centuries was a great increase in population, much greater than had ever been known before. It is probable that this was the result of better medical knowledge, more peaceful conditions and more food production. Probably all these factors contributed to the rise which took place in every country in Europe, both those going through industrial changes and those still rather backward. Examples show that in England in 1700 the population was 6 000 000 and in 1 800, 9 000 000, and in France it was 17 000 000 in 1700 and 26 000 000 in 1800.

Agriculture

Widespread changes took place in agriculture as well as in industry, and we sometimes speak of the 'Agricultural Revolution'. New machines were invented for ploughing, sowing and harvesting and new ideas were tried for using the land to give best results. It was found that by growing a different crop each year for three or four years, the ground could be kept more fertile and better crops could be harvested. This is called the rotation of crops.

View of an industrial city

Viscount Townshend and Arthur Young

Wealthy landlords who were interested in agriculture began to experiment with different crops and different types of seeds and with using machinery in farming so that the work could be done more quickly and efficiently. One English lord called Viscount Townshend was particularly interested in growing turnips so that these could be fed to the cows in the winter months when there was very little for them to eat. He was nicknamed 'Turnip Townshend'. He was also very interested in crop rotation, and he found the following rotation effective in his county of Norfolk. In the first year he grew a root crop, in the second barley, in the third clover and in the fourth year he grew wheat. He found that the root crop cleaned the soil while the clover enriched it with nitrogen compounds. In this way the wheat crops would be of much better quality. Crop rotation was tried in other parts of the country and different systems were found to suit each kind of soil.

Another Englishman who was interested in agriculture was Arthur Young. He did not farm himself, but he travelled around the country talking about farming and telling farmers about new methods that he had seen being used. He also wrote books about agriculture. He was travelling in France just before the French Revolution and noticed the contrast between the English and the French aristocrats. He wrote that the French liked to live at court and were not interested in their lands, whereas the English liked the country and were interested in improving their lands by the newest agricultural methods.

Robert Bakewell

Another important change was the breeding of larger and better quality cows, sheep and horses which Robert Bakewell learned to do. He was careful to allow only the best animals to breed and he fed them well, so that each generation was born bigger and grew up stronger, until the weight of his cows was double that of most cows before his time. Many people were interested in his experiments and those who visited his farm in Leicestershire went away determined to improve their own farms.

Costume

We have seen how England was changed by the Industrial and Agricultural Revolutions. These changes were reflected in the costume of the period. The invention of the spinning frame meant that cotton became cheaper and was available to the poorer people. It was strong, long-lasting. and practical. The rich people dressed in silks and satins and more richly embroidered clothes. Jewels and precious beads were sewn onto dresses and also sometimes onto gloves and shoes.

In the seventeenth century people wore their own hair, usually quite long, but in the eighteenth century there was a fashion for wearing wigs which were powdered with thick white powder. At this time, when both ladies and gentlemen wore wigs, most houses of rich people had powder-rooms, where more powder could be put on their wigs. This made a lot of dust, so a special room was necessary. Judges and lawyers still wear wigs in the law courts.

The French Revolution had a great influence on fashion, not only in France but also in the other countries in Europe. When the King and Queen and the aristocrats were

A satire on ladies' hairstyles in the eighteenth century

Fashion in French revolutionary times

Nineteenth-century clothes showing typical wide skirt

overthrown in France, all citizens in Paris began to wear very simple and inexpensive clothes so that no one would think they belonged to the nobility. The poorer people in Paris did not wear the knee breeches which were worn in the previous century but wore trousers instead, and soon everyone was wearing long trousers. The fashion spread to England, and men in Europe have worn long trousers ever since. As a result of the move towards ordinary wear, men's clothes and women's dresses became more simple.

The style of dress that was fashionable under Napoléon was called 'Empire style'. Both dresses and furniture imitated the style of the Ancient Greeks and Romans. The style spread to other countries too. After the nineteenth century clothes became more formal and stiff. Find pictures of men's and women's costumes during the period 1600 to 1900 and also look at the portraits and paintings of people reproduced throughout this book. Some of the clothes look magnificent; some look a little odd to us now. Which do you think look most comfortable?

Architecture

There were two main trends in architecture during the period of this book. There was the classical style which was favoured by admirers of Greek and Roman Antiquity during the seventeenth and eighteenth century; and there was the Romantic style of the late

The Palace of Versailles

Constable's painting of a study for his masterpiece,, The Haywain

Turner Ship in snow storm

Spring *by Monet*

Boats *by Seurat*

Self-portrait *by Cézanne*

eighteenth and early nineteenth centuries. There are many fine examples of classical architecture. One, St. Paul's Cathedral in London, is shown opposite. It was designed by Sir Christopher Wren as part of a plan to rebuild London after much of it was destroyed by fire in 1666. If you look carefully you can see the influence of the classical style in the columns and the dome. In Germany and Italy the classical style was more ornate, and the fronts of houses and churches were decorated with stone sculpture. Inside were twisted columns, elaborate paintings and a great deal of gold decoration.

Many country mansions were built all over Europe during the eighteenth century. They were designed to look simple but elegant and impressive. They were symmetrical in layout and fitted well into the surrounding countryside. In fact this was such an important part of designing a home that wealthy landowners employed a landscape architect to design the garden as well. The picture shows the palace and gardens at Versailles. Many houses were modelled on Versailles.

The Romantic style of architecture began in England where poets and novelists had already aroused the public's interest in Romanticism. This style took its ideas from the Gothic architecture of the Middle Ages. People started to build houses with small windows, towers, spiral staircases and battlements. Railway stations and town halls started to look a bit like Gothic cathedrals. This style is called neo-Gothic. You can see an example of it below.

St Paul's Cathedral

Furniture

Styles in furniture followed the architecture. In the Classical period of architecture, furniture too was simple and elegant. There were many famous interior designers, but we have picked the work of Robert Adam to show in the picture. Robert and his brother James were from Scotland and lived at the end of the eighteenth century. They are famous not only for their furniture but for the wonderful interiors — fireplaces, mirrors and mouldings — that they designed.

In the nineteenth century, people packed their neo-Gothic houses full of furniture. All the romantic little rooms had to have sofas, chairs, books and musical instruments in them. The walls were covered with small

St Pancras station

An Adam interior

A Victorian study

pictures or prints, and plants stood on the tables. The people of the nineteenth century wanted to be surrounded by objects; it was partly to show that they could afford to have so many. Many people had grown rich because of industrialisation and they used their homes to prove their wealth.

Music

The development of music through the three centuries of this book runs parallel with the making of new and more powerful musical instruments. At the beginning of the sixteenth century musicians in Europe played instruments like the harpsichord and lute which do not have a very strong sound. They played together in a group called a consort. Well brought-up ladies and gentlemen were expected to master one or two instruments. By the end of the nineteenth century the piano had been invented and there was a whole new set of instruments in the brass and percussion sections. Trumpets, trombones and horns were now part of every orchestra. Composers wrote for large concert halls rather than for a room in someone's home.

Most new music was commissioned by the Church to be sung in cathedrals. This is called choral music because it is a combination of choir and orchestra. One of the greatest writers of choral music was Johann Sebastian Bach who lived in Germany at the end of the seventeenth century and the beginning of the eighteenth century. One of his best known works, the St. Matthew Passion, tells of the coming of Christ to the world and of his death and resurrection. Bach set the words from the St. Matthew Gospel to music. Bach also wrote non-religious music which could be played by small orchestras or groups of players. This is called chamber music because it can be played in a chamber (room). A typical piece of chamber music would have one or two violins, violas, a cello, harpsichord and maybe a flute or a clarinet. Another well-known composer of chamber music, and of operas, was Henry Purcell who lived in England a little before Bach's time. An opera is a play which is acted on a stage, but the words are sung instead of spoken. Purcell's operas were light entertainment. *The Fairy Queen* is one of them; it uses the plot of Shakespeare's play, *A Midsummer Night's Dream.*

A group of chamber musicians

It was really Mozart and Verdi who developed the opera into a fine art. In both their works, the music communicates much more to the listener than the words or actions. The music tells us what the characters in the drama feel — whether it is happiness or sadness. Wolfgang Amadeus Mozart was born in Austria at the end of the eighteenth century. He was a brilliant piano player as a child and when he was six his father took him on a tour of other European countries. He remained a great musician all his life and has given us some wonderful music, chamber music, religious works and operas. Try to listen to his opera *The Marriage of Figaro* which is a story about the privileges of an aristocrat and how he treats his servants. It was written shortly before the French Revolution and contains the kind of social criticism which was to lead to revolution and change.

Another composer who was critical of social and political events was the German composer Ludwig van Beethoven. He lived through the restless period of the French Revolution and the subsequent upheavals under Napoléon Bonaparte. He was a restless, temperamental man who was rarely happy. He wrote some very fine, mature music mainly for piano and for symphony orchestra. His ninth, and last, symphony has singers and a choir in the last movement. It is a rare build-up of glorious sound and was unlike anything written before. Beethoven's tragedy was that he was going deaf towards the end of his life. He did not hear his ninth symphony when it was played but he was such a good musician that he knew what it would sound like.

Richard Wagner learned a great deal from Beethoven. He too was a German and he lived at the end of the nineteenth century. He lived at a time when nationalism was strong in Europe and his music reflects this. The German people found his works an inspiration. His long operas are still very popular today even though they are difficult to perform. *The Ring* is a series of five operas about heroes and gods of ancient mythology. Wagner's music is very grand and uses a large orchestra.

Painting

Nature

In the eighteenth century there was a new interest in the countryside and in nature. Instead of being the background of a picture, the landscape became the picture itself, and the figures became small and insignificant. Painters were interested in the effects of clouds, water and mist, the light on hills and streams. Constable painted peaceful country scenes and was particularly noted for his painting of trees. Turner was fascinated by the effect of light on water and painted vivid, imaginative pictures of storms and rainbows, sea battles, and even railway trains in the early nineteenth century.

Impressionism

At the end of the nineteenth century a group of French painters began to paint an impression of what they saw instead of trying to paint what they actually saw. They seemed to see shapes and colours much more vividly than they actually were and so their paintings glowed with bright colours. Monet, Renoir and Cézanne were the most well known of these painters. Monet painted many pictures of a cathedral in different lights and later painted huge pictures of water lilies. Renoir painted soft, romantic pictures of the people he saw in Paris society and particularly of young girls. Cézanne was fascinated by shapes of objects and geometrical shapes.

Four impressionist painters stand out for their uses of colour. Van Gogh was a Dutchman who settled in France and painted vivid pictures of people and the countryside. Gauguin settled in Tahiti in the South Pacific and painted the people of the island. Matisse was most interested in colours and the effects caused by putting certain colours next to each other, especially red and green. Another painter, Seurat, was interested in new developments in photography. He noticed that colour photographs were made up of tiny dots so he painted his pictures in dots of colour to see what effect this would have. This kind of painting is called 'pointillisme'. The impressionists were very much influenced by photography because it challenged the value of painting. If photographs could reproduce people and places exactly,

Matisse: Portrait of a woman

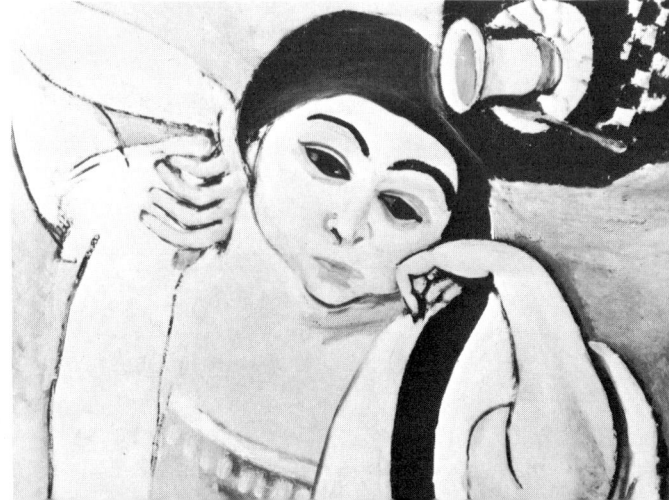

then painting had to do something else. It had to portray the character or impression of the subject.

Literature

Literature, like music, was at first very much involved with religious thought. Later it became a comment on social life. *Pilgrim's Progress*, a great religious work, was written by John Bunyan while he was in prison in the late seventeenth century. It tells the story of a Christian's journey through life, and of his exciting and dangerous adventures before he reaches Heaven. It is a story of great courage in face of temptations and trouble, and has inspired people ever since.

We know a great deal about life in England during the eighteenth and nineteenth centuries from novels, or stories about people and everyday life at the time. *Tom Jones* was written by Henry Fielding in the middle of the eighteenth century and was the story of a lively young man and his adventures through life. In the early nineteenth century Jane Austen wrote sensitive and delightful novels about the society in which she lived. It was so unusual for a woman to write books that she published them anonymously.

A few years later three sisters, Charlotte, Anne and Emily Brontë were writing books. The greatest of these were *Wuthering Heights* by Emily, and *Jane Eyre* by Charlotte.

Another woman who wrote novels took the name of George Eliot in order to hide the fact that she was a woman. Her books included *Middlemarch, Silas Marner* and *Adam Bede.*

Charles Dickens described life in nineteenth century London in a series of novels which have become famous throughout the world, particularly *David Copperfield, Nicholas Nickleby* and *The Pickwick Papers.* He wrote one story called *A Christmas Carol* about a mean and miserly man called Scrooge, who was visited by a ghost and persuaded to change his character and be generous and kind.

Things To Do

1 Make a list of famous scientists and find out more about each one from an encyclopaedia or book of reference.

2 Make a model of Arkwright's spinning frame.

3 Write a paragraph explaining the importance of the invention of the steam engine. Find out if steam engines are still used today.

4 Make drawings to show the changes in men's or women's costume between A.D. 1700 and 1900.

5 Draw or photograph a local building which you think has been influenced by Classical or Gothic style.

6 Listen to some music by some of the composers mentioned.

7 Look at paintings by some of the painters mentioned. Choose one picture that you like and try to write a description of it.

8 Read some of the novels mentioned in the section on literature.

6
The Commonwealth

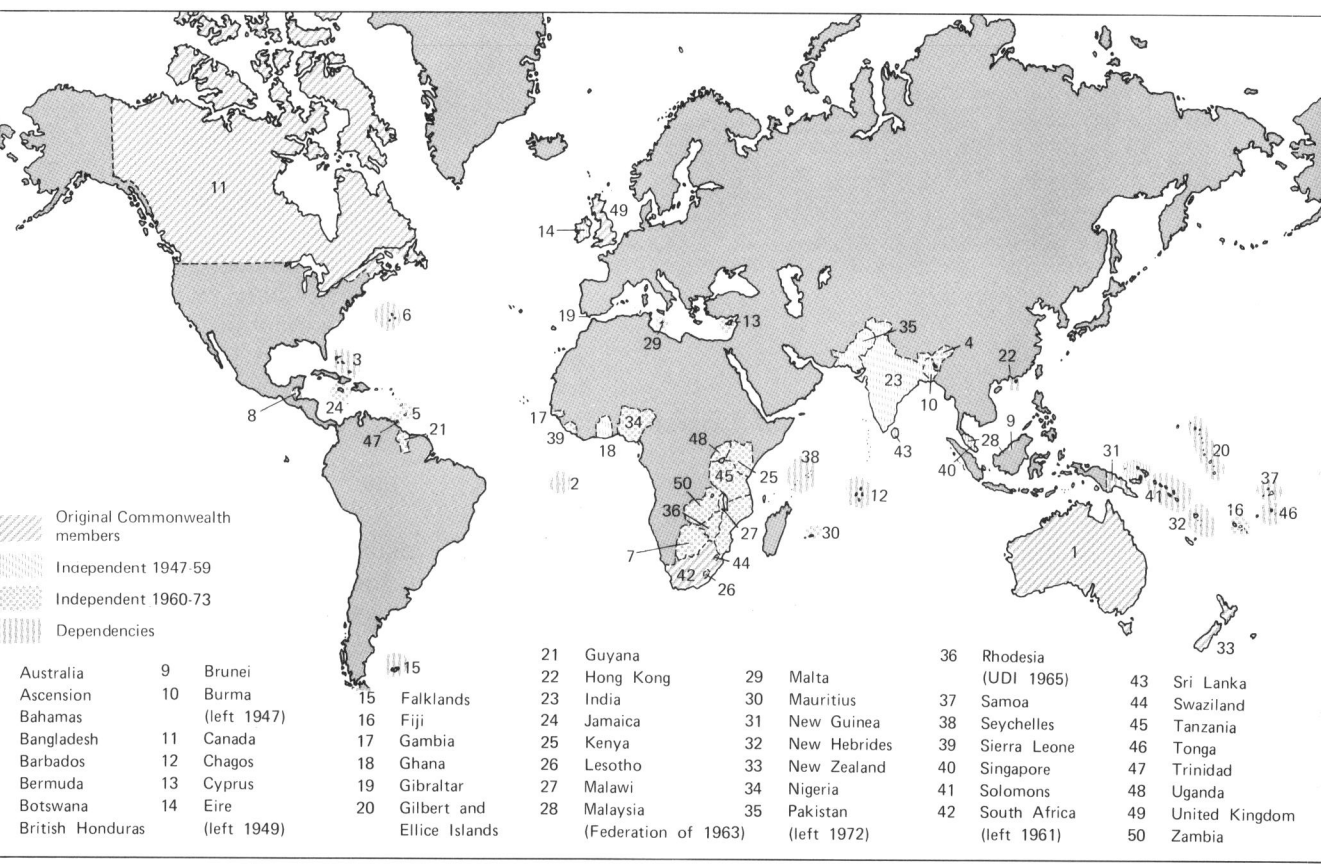

Original Commonwealth members

Independent 1947-59

Independent 1960-73

Dependencies

Australia		9	Brunei		21	Guyana	36	Rhodesia
Ascension		10	Burma		22	Hong Kong	29 Malta	(UDI 1965)
Bahamas			(left 1947)	15	Falklands	23	India	30 Mauritius	37 Samoa
Bangladesh		11	Canada	16	Fiji	24	Jamaica	31 New Guinea	38 Seychelles
Barbados		12	Chagos	17	Gambia	25	Kenya	32 New Hebrides	39 Sierra Leone
Bermuda		13	Cyprus	18	Ghana	26	Lesotho	33 New Zealand	40 Singapore
Botswana		14	Eire	19	Gibraltar	27	Malawi	34 Nigeria	41 Solomons
British Honduras			(left 1949)	20	Gilbert and	28	Malaysia	35 Pakistan	42 South Africa
					Ellice Islands		(Federation of 1963)	(left 1972)	(left 1961)

43	Sri Lanka
44	Swaziland
45	Tanzania
46	Tonga
47	Trinidad
48	Uganda
49	United Kingdom
50	Zambia

Map of the Commonwealth

The Commonwealth is a free association of independent states. They are situated in all the continents of the world and contain peoples of all races and religions. All of them were once ruled by Britain, but they are now of equal importance with Britain when their leaders meet together. English is used as the common language between the member countries although it may not be their first language. Some of them are republics, others monarchies, others military dictatorships, but all of them recognise the king or queen of the United Kingdom as head of the Commonwealth. Their leaders meet together, usually once a year, to discuss problems and difficulties. If any member country wishes to leave the Commonwealth, it is free to do so. Four countries, Burma, Eire, South Africa and Pakistan have done this.

The British Empire

The Commonwealth grew out of the British Empire, an overseas empire which Britain gained mainly during the eighteenth and nineteenth centuries. The first nations to gain independent or 'Dominion' status were Canada, Australia, New Zealand and South Africa. They had reached this stage before the First World War. Since then, many other nations have become independent. By 1973 there were thirty-three full members of the Commonwealth.

An early settlement in Virginia

The Beginning

The British Empire began with a number of small colonies – overseas settlements by people from Britain. The first of these colonies was one called Virginia in North America in the early seventeenth century.

Other colonies were founded by people who were persecuted because of their religious views. A group of Puritans called the Pilgrim Fathers settled in New England, much further north, while a group of Roman Catholics settled in Maryland, and a group of Quakers settled in Pennsylvania. Gradually the colonies grew and developed into self-reliant and determined groups all along the east coast of America.

French settlers occupied part of Canada, but when Britain defeated France in war in the middle of the eighteenth century, these French-speaking colonists came under British rule. Much of Canada is still French-speaking.

The American Revolution

The English colonists in America objected when Britain tried to make them pay taxes. 'No taxation without representation' they said. They did not see why they should pay taxes when they were not represented in Parliament in England. The British government then tried to make them pay taxes on legal documents and on tea which was imported from India. The colonists were so angry that they threw the tea into the harbour at Boston, and war started between them and the British government in 1774. After some years of fighting, during which they were led by George Washington, the colonists won their independence from Britain. They called themselves the United States of America, and drew up a Constitution. We shall read about this in Chapter 7. From this time they were quite separate from Britain and from the British Empire.

The British had, however, learned not to be too severe with their colonies, and when the Canadians rose in revolt in 1837, the British government considered their problems sympathetically, and granted them much more independence and self-government instead of trying to force them into obedience. In this way Canada became the first dominion.

The West Indies

Some of the oldest members of the Commonwealth are the islands of Bermuda, St. Kitts, Barbados and the Bahamas. Most of the islands in the West Indies grew sugar and tobacco, and slaves were brought from Africa to work there. When the slaves were freed in 1833, some of the planters brought in Indians and Chinese labourers to work instead. People of many races now live together in the West Indies.

There were two British territories on the mainland, British Honduras in Central America, and British Guiana on the coast of South America. France, Spain and Holland also had colonies in the West Indies.

Fathers of the Confederation in London

Captain Cook in the South Seas

Australia and New Zealand

Captain James Cook explored the coasts of Australia and New Zealand during the years 1768–70 and reported that the land was fertile. Ten years later the British government sent one thousand convicts, people who had been sentenced in law courts, to settle in Australia. It was difficult at first, but gradually more and more settlements were made, some of convicts, and others of free men. Sheep farming developed well and when gold was discovered in various places, people rushed to Australia in the hope of getting rich quickly. The native people of Australia, called aborigines, were a very primitive people. Their hunting grounds were taken away from them; many of them caught diseases from the colonists and their numbers went down rapidly.

The native people of New Zealand, called Maoris, were more advanced and had learned how to farm the land. Missionaries converted them to Christianity and persuaded them to co-operate with the British government, and New Zealand became a British colony. There were troubles and, sometimes, even fights between the Maoris and the settlers, but gradually they settled down to develop the country peacefully.

The Pacific Islands

Some of the islands in the Pacific became British, including the Gilbert and Ellice Islands, Fiji and Tonga. France and Germany and other countries were also involved and gained Pacific Islands. After the First World War the German territories were governed by Britain or Australia.

India

The trade routes from Europe to India and the Far East were discovered by the Portuguese, but merchants from other European countries soon began to sail round the Cape of Good Hope towards India in search of trade. They formed trade companies and established trading posts where they built warehouses for storing their goods until the ships came. English, French and Dutch merchants as well as Portuguese took part in this trade. India was divided into many states, each ruled by a prince. In the seventeenth century north India had been ruled by Muslim princes from their capital in Delhi. After that time the control of the Muslim princes became weaker and weaker. The English and French trading companies found

British sailors hoist the flag in Australia

themselves taking control of large areas of India in order to keep peaceful trade going. When the English fought the French and took Canada, they also took some of the French possessions in India. By the end of the eighteenth century the British were in control of India. It became such an important part of the British Empire that it was regarded as an empire in itself.

The British in India

Gandhi

The Mutiny

In 1857 India was still ruled by the East India Company — a private British trading company. In that year many of the Indian soldiers who were in the company's army rebelled. One of the reasons for their rebellion was the grease that they had to use for their guns. The Hindus were angry because they thought it was cow fat, and they believe that the cow is sacred. The Muslims were angry because they thought it was pig fat and they believe that the pig is unclean. There was bitter and savage fighting and terrible punishment. The British government abolished the East India Company and began to govern India itself. Queen Victoria became the Empress of India. Ceylon and Burma also formed part of the Indian Empire.

Gandhi

In the early twentieth century there was a great Indian leader, Gandhi. Gandhi believed in helping people in any way he could. He set up a community of people who lived and worked together in a spirit of love and truth. There were no differences among them in

the work they did or the food they ate. They lived a very simple life following Gandhi's ideas. He travelled about India encouraging people to refuse to co-operate with the British if they were being maltreated. He was very concerned for the Untouchables, people who did the worst jobs and who could not use the same transport, wells or temples as other people. Gandhi decided to fast to death unless the Untouchables were included as voters for the Parliament that India was to have. His wish was granted and the position of the Untouchables improved a great deal.

Gandhi also tried very hard to heal the differences between the Hindus and the Muslims, but, in spite of all his appeals, there was bitter fighting in 1946, just before India became independent. Two separate states were set up, a Muslim state of Pakistan and a largely Hindu state of India. For many years these states were on the verge of war. In 1971 East Pakistan wanted to become independent, and India won a war against West Pakistan; India helped East Pakistan to become the independent country, Bangladesh; Pakistan then chose to leave the Commonwealth.

Malaysia

The East India Company, which had been responsible for the development of trading posts in India, sent ships further east to explore the possibilities of trade in South-east Asia. Trading posts were set up along the coast of Malaya, at Penang, Malacca and Singapore. Malaya was divided into separate states, each ruled by a Malay Muslim prince. Many of them accepted a British adviser, and gradually the whole of the Malay Peninsula came under British 'protection'. Tin and rubber industries developed, and Chinese labourers came to work in the tin mines or on the rubber plantations.

Hong Kong harbour in 1870

Sarawak

The Sultan of Brunei on the island of Borneo asked the East India Company for help in controlling the pirates along the coast. The man who achieved this was called James Brooke. The Sultan rewarded him by making him ruler or Rajah of the whole of Sarawak. James Brooke and his family continued to rule Sarawak until 1946. They were called the White Rajahs. Another British Company of traders ruled North Borneo (Sabah). Today Sabah and Sarawak form part of the state of Malaysia, but Singapore is a separate state.

Hong Kong

British merchants had great difficulty in trading with China because the Chinese government wanted to limit and restrict foreign trade as much as possible, particularly as much of the trade was in opium, which British and other merchants brought from India and sold in China. War broke out between Britain and China. In 1841 the British merchants were no longer able to stay in Canton, so they moved to the island of Hong Kong, and Captain Elliott took possession of the island. In 1842, China ceded Hong Kong to Britain; Kowloon was added in 1860. No one at that time had any idea that it would become such a successful trading place. Gradually more and more people, Chinese, Indian, Portuguese and English, came to live in Hong Kong and developed trade there. The British government obtained a lease of the hinterland, that is, the New Territories and the off-shore islands, in 1898.

The British in Sarawak with Rajah Brooke

61

The Boers in South Africa

South Africa

South Africa was first settled by Dutchmen, but, during the wars against Napoléon, Britain took possession of the Cape of Good Hope, where the Dutch had settled. The Dutch settlers, called Boers, did not like the British rule, so they trekked or travelled northwards and set up two states called the Orange Free State and the Transvaal.

Quite soon diamonds were discovered in the Transvaal and many Europeans went there to work in the diamond mines. The Boers did not like all these people coming, and treated them badly. Meanwhile, many English people had settled in the Cape and some of them wanted to extend British power over the Boer States. Cecil Rhodes was already interested in developing the area to the north-east of the Transvaal, which is today called Rhodesia, and he wanted to link this up with the Cape. From 1899 to 1902 there was a war between the Boers of the Transvaal and the British government, and the Boers were defeated. The British government did their best afterwards to help the Boers recover and allowed the four states of South Africa (Transvaal, Orange Free State, Natal and the Cape) to gain self-government very quickly. Unfortunately, the British government did not insist that there should eventually be equal rights for the African people.

Since independence the government of South Africa has kept the power in the hands of the European settlers and has not allowed the African people to have any share. In fact the government of South Africa has developed a policy of apartheid, or separate development for people of different races. As the other Commonwealth countries disapproved strongly of this policy, South Africa withdrew from the Commonwealth in 1960.

Central Africa

Three British colonies were established in this area, Northern Rhodesia, Southern Rhodesia and Nyasaland. They were joined together in a Federation after the Second World War, but the Federation did not last long because of the different interests and ideas of the three countries. Northern Rhodesia became independent as Zambia, and Nyasaland as Malawi, while Southern Rhodesia remained a colony, called Rhodesia. Rhodesia declared itself independent of Britain in 1965, without Britain's agreement. The white Rhodesians, who are the minority, have all the power and wish to keep it. Britain wants progress towards majority rule.

Black and white Rhodesians in a multi-racial bar

East Africa

Kenya and Uganda became British colonies and Tanganyika became a British mandate after the First World War. Later, the island of Zanzibar joined with Tanganyika to form the independent state of Tanzania, while Kenya and Uganda also became independent.

West Africa

Very few English people went to live in West Africa because they found that they were unsuited to the climate and the tropical diseases were fatal. By the end of the nineteenth century, however, four British colonies had been set up. They were Ghana, Nigeria, Gambia and Sierra Leone. Sierra Leone was established in the early nineteenth century as a place to which freed slaves from America could come if they wanted to return to Africa. The most important town was called Freetown. France, Portugal and Germany also had colonies along the west coast and the boundaries between the colonies did not usually correspond with the area where different African tribes lived. Nigeria contained at least three very different groups of African tribes and it was difficult for the state to remain united after it had gained its independence in 1960.

North Africa

The whole of the North African coast had once formed part of the Turkish Empire, but by the nineteenth century that Empire was so weak that the Sultan could not resist the attempts of the European nations to gain control of the area. France was particularly concerned because she was herself a Mediterranean power and did a great deal of trade in the Mediterranean Sea. She gained control of Algeria, Tunis and Morocco, in spite of attempts by Germany to stop her. England was more interested in Egypt because of her communications with India. When the Suez Canal was built in 1869, this became the shortest route to India. France and England together took control of Egyptian finances as the situation in Egypt was so confused, but France soon withdrew and left England to establish a Protectorate over Egypt and the Sudan.

Other Territories and Islands

Britain took possession of many islands and land bases to protect her sea routes. Some of these are Malta and Gibraltar and Cyprus in the Mediterranean; Ascension, St. Helena and Tristan da Cunha in the South Atlantic; Mauritius and the Seychelles in the Indian Ocean, and the Falkland Islands off the tip of

Commonwealth conference in Singapore, 1971

South America. It is difficult for such small islands and territories to be economically independent. Some of them, like Gibraltar, are wanted by their neighbours. Spain would like to take over Gibraltar, but the people of Gibraltar do not want this; they want to remain British.

Most of the independent members of the Commonwealth are also members of the United Nations and take a full part in world affairs.

Things To Do

1 Find out as much as you can about the Commonwealth today and the present leaders of the member states. Ask the British Council or write to The Commonwealth Institute, Kensington High Street, London W8, England, or any British information service.

2 Find out the population, geography, climate, races, languages and special features or problems of each member state of the Commonwealth and of the remaining dependencies. Prepare short talks or essays, and collect information for a chart. This can be done as a class project for individual or group work.

3 Find out more about Gandhi.

4 Keep a book of newspaper cuttings about modern developments in the Commonwealth.

5 Write a short project on one of the following subjects:

the American colonies   Australia
the West Indies   South Africa

You should find out the history of the place you have chosen. Illustrate your project with drawings.

6 Imagine that you were an Untouchable in India. Write a story about a day in your life.

7
The United States of America

Independence

When the thirteen colonies in North America won their independence from Britain in 1783 they were granted the land from the Atlantic to the Mississippi river including a large area of land to the south of the great lakes. This area is shown on the map on page 67. Their first task was to decide how to govern themselves and the territories they had been granted. Each of the colonies had different interests and different ideas and it was difficult for them to agree on a constitution for them all. During the summer of 1787 representatives from all the colonies, or states as they now called themselves, met in Philadelphia to discuss the problem. They soon decided to write a new Constitution for the thirteen states and any future states that might be added. When it was finished each state had the opportunity to discuss it and decide whether they approved or not. Most of the states favoured the Constitution, but a few of them wanted more protection of the freedom of the individual, so they added some clauses, which were called amendments, to the Constitution.

The Constitution of the United States of America starts like this:

'We, the people of the United States, in order to form a more perfect union, establish justice, insure domestic tranquillity, provide for the common defence, promote the general welfare, and secure the blessings of liberty to ourselves and our posterity, do ordain and establish this Constitution for the United States of America.'

The Constitution described exactly how the United States were to be governed, and how much power the central, or federal, government would have and how much was left to the individual states. This Constitution has lasted basically unchanged but with many amendments to the present day.

Federal and State Government

A system of government was set up which is still in existence. There was a central authority called the federal government and there were the individual state governments. The federal government consists of a president and Congress. Congress is made up of the Senate and the House of Representatives, both elected by the people. The president is elected by the people for a four-year term. The federal government made the laws and saw that they were carried out, and decided

New York in the eighteenth century

foreign policy, trade and taxation issues. Each state was allowed to choose its own representatives to deal with local affairs such as education, housing and marriage laws.

George Washington

The first president of the United States was George Washington, who had been commander-in-chief of the army during the War of Independence. He had led his army through great hardship and danger to final victory, and he now took the position of president and did his best to make sure that the new Constitution was put into practice. In 1789 he took the oath that every president since that time has taken at the inaugural (opening) ceremony:

> 'I do solemnly swear that I will faithfully execute the office of president of the United States, and will to the best of my ability, preserve, protect and defend the Constitution of the United States.'

As he bent to kiss the Bible over which he had taken the oath, the people shouted, 'Long live George Washington, president of the United States.'

Washington at the inaugural ceremony

The people of the United States respected and admired Washington and he set a good example of how a president should act. He was wise and dignified, and chose the best men to advise him in his job. He held office for two terms and only retired to his country home in Mount Vernon, Virginia, in 1797. Before retiring, he made a speech advising Americans to avoid getting involved in 'entangling alliances' in Europe, and to try not to let political differences at home seriously divide them. The capital city of the United States was named after Washington.

Thomas Jefferson

Washington's chief adviser on foreign policy was Thomas Jefferson. He was responsible for writing the Declaration of Independence of 1776 which stated why the colonies should be independent of Britain. During Washington's presidency Jefferson favoured helping the French revolutionaries because their ideas of government and liberty were similar to those of the United States. However, Washington wisely decided that it would be better for the United States not to become involved in the war between the revolutionaries and the other countries of Europe. However, America did join the First World War, towards the end, in 1917.

Thomas Jefferson was elected president in 1801 and governed until 1809. By this time the situation in France had changed because Napoléon had seized power, and Jefferson now felt it was right to keep out of European affairs. At home Jefferson believed strongly in the rights and freedom of the individual so that people sometimes describe his time as 'Jeffersonian Democracy'.

Thomas Jefferson

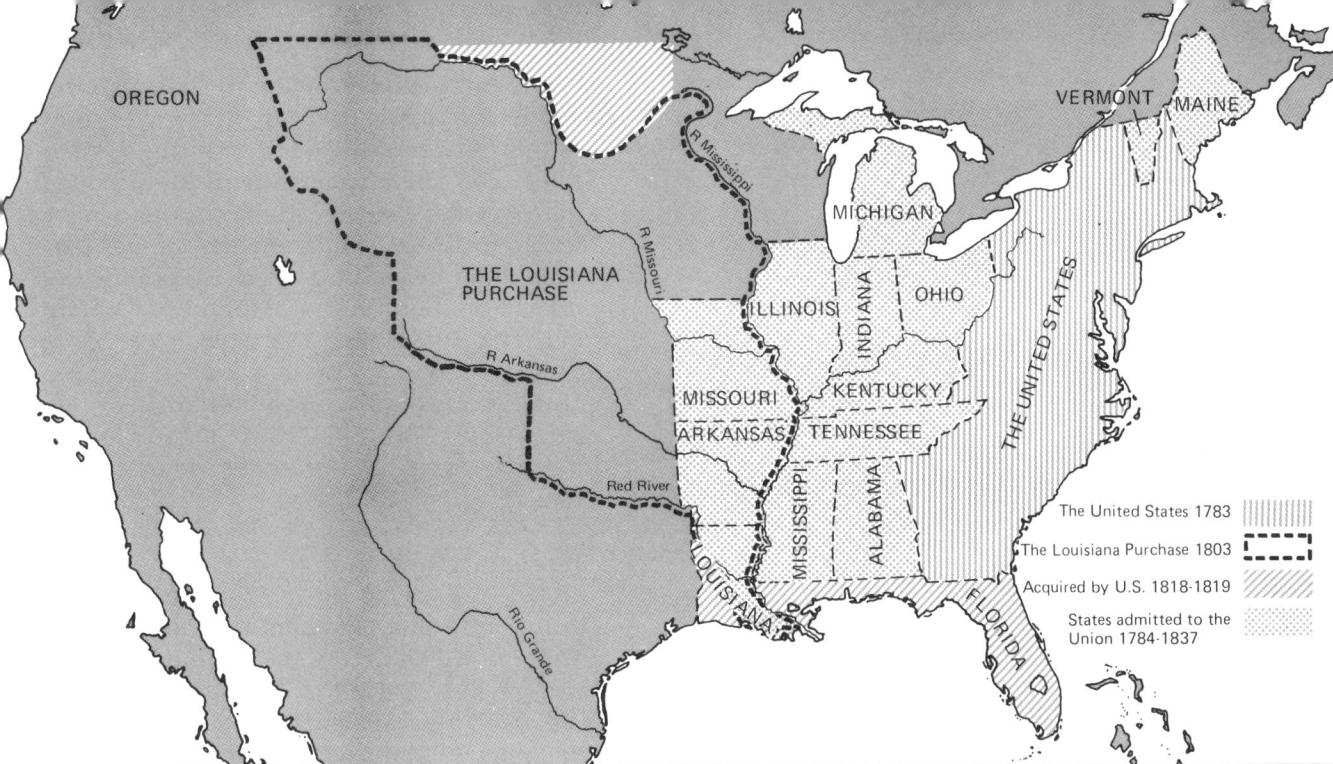

The expanding frontier

The Louisiana Purchase

When Napoléon conquered Spain he also took over Spanish territory in North America which included large areas of land west of the Mississippi river. Jefferson was very worried about this as he was afraid that the ambitious Napoléon might try to re-establish a French Empire in North America. However, Napoléon had enough problems at home, so he was quite willing to sell the whole of Louisiana to the United States. Louisiana was the area between New Orleans and the British territories in Canada. The Louisiana Purchase of 1803 doubled the size of the United States and provided much more land for settlers to develop agriculturally. Jefferson sent two men called Lewis and Clark to explore the new land in 1804. They traced the Missouri River to its source and then found a route across the Rocky Mountains to the Pacific Ocean through the territory of Oregon.

The Mexican War

The boundary between the United States and Canada was decided peacefully by negotiation and there has never been any serious fighting between the two. To the south-west, however, there were disputes over the territory between the Pacific Ocean and the Gulf of Mexico which was owned by Mexico. Mexico had been a Spanish colony, but she gained her independence at the beginning of the nineteenth century.

Many Americans who came into the United States at the time of the Louisiana Purchase went further west and explored Texas and California. Some of them settled there, but they longed to be ruled by their own countrymen and not by the Mexicans. Those who had settled in Texas declared their independence, but at the famous battle of the Alamo, in which Davy Crockett became so well known, they were defeated by the Mexicans. For ten years Texas was known as the Lone Star Republic and its independence was generally recognised. In 1845 the Congress of the United States decided to admit Texas to the Union and so Texas became the twenty-eighth state.

Congress continued to try to increase their territory and tried to buy California and New

Digging for gold in California

Pioneers going westwards

Mexico but the government of Mexico, who owned the land, refused, so a war was fought between Mexico and the United States. The United States won the war and took over the lands of California and New Mexico in 1848. After a while gold was discovered in California and hundreds of prospectors hurried to California to look for gold. This was called the Gold Rush. As a result of this, California soon had a big enough population to be admitted as a state of the United States in 1850. It took longer to settle the other territories gained from Mexico.

The Westward Movement

Throughout the nineteenth century many people travelled across the United States to look for new places to live or to hunt for gold. These people faced great dangers of attack by Indians and bandits as well as great hardships from the climate and the difficulty of the journeys. When they found land and settled, they had to build their own houses and make all their own furniture and everything that they needed. Life was very difficult, particularly for the women and children. People became independent and able to live on their own. When railways and better roads were built in the second half of the nineteenth century, conditions became a little better, and the farmers had more opportunities to sell and export their products.

Thousands of new immigrants came from Europe to the United States during the nineteenth century to find political or religious freedom, or just to try to have a better life and escape from the poverty of their life in Europe. Some of the immigrants worked in factories in the east, but many of them soon began to move westwards in the hope of better prospects. Immigrants also came from Asia, including many large groups from China, in order to work in the mines of California. The conditions and wages of these Chinese workers were sometimes very bad, and so lowered the standard of living of the others that finally the government had to try to stop this kind of immigration. Today the United States is composed of people of

The Americans in New England fight against English forces in the War of Independence

Building a railway line in the Far West

British settlers set up their camp in South Africa

Native Hottentots in Africa

These were the people Captain Cook saw in Australia

A battle between Captain Cook and native Australians. Captain Cook is wounded and dies

East India Company ships set out for a trading voyage

The Declaration of Independence

A rising city in the west

many different races, and from many different countries, but all speak English and consider themselves American citizens.

The Mormons

The early nineteenth century was a time of intense religious revival and many societies were formed. In 1823 a youth of eighteen named Joseph Smith declared that he had seen an angel who encouraged him to found a new religion. The angel, who was called Moroni, dictated to him a book which was engraved on gold plates. Three witnesses swore that they had seen the plates and agreed to follow Joseph Smith. He called the book the Book of Mormon and the religion he founded was known as Mormon or the Church of Jesus Christ of the Latter-day Saints. He soon had many followers, but there were also many people who did not approve of the new religion and so Joseph Smith decided to move westwards with his converts. However, in 1844, Joseph Smith was murdered but, under the leadership of one of his followers, a city was finally built in Utah, near the Great Salt Lake. At first, the Federal Government refused to make Utah into a state of the Union. Finally, when various unpopular laws were abolished,

Utah was admitted as the forty-fifth state. This was in 1896. The story of the Mormons shows how pioneer groups opened up the land in the mid-west of America and created new states.

The Civil War

In Congress northern and southern states found it difficult to agree. Whenever a new state was created in the north, the southerners pressed for a new one in the south to balance it. The reason for this was that the northern states were industrial and the southern were mainly agricultural and so there was economic rivalry between them. In the southern states of the United States cotton and tobacco plantations were bringing large profits to the rich plantation owners who employed negro slaves to work on their plantations.

These negroes had been brought from Africa by ship during the seventeenth and eighteenth centuries. The conditions on the ships were so bad that many of them died on the way, and the survivors were sold as slaves at public markets. More and more people realised that slavery was wrong and that slaves ought to be set free. They were

73

called 'abolitionists' because they wanted to abolish slavery. In the British Empire the slave trade was stopped in 1807 and slavery itself abolished in 1833. But in America it was difficult for the southern planters to think of setting free their slaves because they thought it would be impossible to continue farming without slave labour. Many northerners, however, began to make speeches and write books urging that slavery should be abolished.

Harriet Beecher Stowe wrote a book called *Uncle Tom's Cabin* describing the hardships faced by Uncle Tom, a negro slave in the south. The book was very popular and made more and more people in the north conscious of the need to abolish slavery. A new political party grew up called the Republican Party. This party was determined to prevent slavery being extended to the territories of the Louisiana Purchase and the lands won from Mexico. One of the most lively speakers of this party was a young lawyer called Abraham Lincoln. He was convinced that slavery would have to be abolished sooner or later but even more important, he thought, was the need to keep the United States united.

South Carolina leaves the Union

The leaders of the southern states, and particularly South Carolina, were afraid that the northerners would force them to liberate their slaves, and they felt that their trading interests were not considered carefully enough by the Federal Government. When Abraham Lincoln was elected president in 1860 the state of South Carolina immediately left the Union. This was called 'seceding from the Union'. Ten other states of the south followed the example of South Carolina and the United States were split in two parts, the North and the South. The southern states called themselves the Confederacy.

Many years earlier George Washington had foreseen the end of slavery. 'I can clearly foresee that nothing but the rooting out of slavery can perpetuate the existence of our union, by consolidating it in a common bond of principle.' Lincoln held similar views: 'A house divided against itself cannot stand; I believe this government cannot permanently endure half slave and half free. I do not expect the Union to be dissolved; I do not expect the house to fall . . . but I do expect it will cease to be divided.'

A slave auction in Virginia

Northern Victory

As president, Lincoln could not accept the secession of the south and when southern men attacked the fortress of Charleston, Lincoln ordered Federal soldiers to move into the south. This was the beginning of a four-year civil war ending in 1865 with the northern victory. Most of the fighting took place in the east near to the northern capital of Washington, and the southern capital of Richmond. General Robert E. Lee of the south was so brilliant a commander that he nearly defeated the north in the first two years of the war, but eventually the north won because they had more men, money, and industrial and agricultural resources. The north set up a sea blockade of the southern ports to prevent the south exporting goods or importing supplies from Europe, but some southern ships managed to get through the blockade. The north were very angry when two ships left England where they had been ordered and brought help to the south.

The End of Slavery

As the northern armies marched into the southern states, plantation slaves ran away from their homes and joined the armies. In 1863 Lincoln proclaimed the emancipation of the slaves, which meant that all slaves were freed. Later an amendment was added to the Constitution confirming that slavery was abolished throughout the United States of America. A few days after the south had surrendered to the north, Lincoln was attending a theatre in Washington when he was shot dead by an assassin. The whole nation was horrified and shocked by this tragedy.

Reconstruction

Lincoln had been determined to re-unite the north and the south as quickly and peacefully as possible, and his successor, Andrew Johnson, tried to carry out Lincoln's ideas, but there was opposition. There were many people in the north who wanted to punish the south and make sure that the north

Abraham Lincoln is shot at the theatre

would continue to dominate the United States. They were called Radical Republicans and they were so strong in Congress that they forced through a very severe plan of reconstruction for the south, enforcing immediate political and civil rights for the negroes and taking the power away from the previous leaders. However, later, the negroes lost their rights and the white southerners regained control. In the twentieth century there has been another attempt to get full civil rights and educational opportunities for the negroes, which we call the Civil Rights Movement. These aims have still not been achieved all over the world. During the time of President Kennedy and President Johnson, Congress passed acts to help the negroes.

Industrialisation

Some of the liberated slaves went into industry after the Civil War, as they wanted to get away from the cotton plantations where they had been made so miserable. So industry increased, especially in the north. Oil drilling and processing became the main industry in Cleveland, Ohio, where the Standard Oil Company was founded. Pittsburg became the centre for steel and set up the United States Steel Corporation. In fact these cities held the monopoly for their two products. This means that they took over all other companies or made them go out of business. Monopolies have certain disadvantages because it can mean that the standard of the goods produced is lowered by the lack of competition. The government tried to control some of the large monopolies, but with only limited success.

During the nineteenth century America grew from being a largely agricultural nation to being an important industrial nation. She grew very wealthy because she had rich industrial resources, such as oil and minerals, and much fertile agricultural land which could produce all the food that her people needed. Immigrants arriving from Europe or the Far East provided labour for the factories on the east coast. However, the conditions in the factories were sometimes very bad and the hours of work very long.

Communications

The United States of America had grown to such a size that it became increasingly important to establish good communications both for trade and government. Gradually a network of railways spread over the whole country. In 1869 the Union Pacific and the Central Pacific Railroads were joined at Ogdon, Utah, and so for the first time trains could run from the east coast all the way to the west — a distance of over 2500 miles. Most of the railways were built by private companies, but the federal government did grant land and lend money to the companies.

Although canals had been built in the United States before railways, they were used less than the railways as a means of transport. The most ambitious canal project attempted by American engineers was the Panama Canal, connecting the Pacific with the Caribbean Sea. The United States encouraged the Panamanian rebellion and then immediately recognised it as a new state, whereupon they built the canal which was finished in 1914.

United States Foreign Policy

In spite of Washington's advice to keep out of European affairs, the United States has been involved in the two World Wars of the twentieth century. In each case she was very reluctant to fight, but trading interests had made closer ties with other countries. As business developed, there was a need for more raw materials from abroad, and more markets for American products. This led to an interest first in the countries of Central and South America, and later in Europe and the Far East. Business interests encouraged the United States government to take a more active interest in foreign affairs.

The Spanish-American War

As America's interest abroad increased, her desire to build an empire also grew. The first opportunity came when the United States was able to take over the Hawaiian

The completion of the Pacific railroad

islands and part of Samoa in 1898–99. The greatest gain came after a fight for independence broke out in Cuba. Cuba was Spanish-owned and was one of the last territories of the Spanish Empire. The Spanish government took steps to put down the rebellion and the Americans were so appalled by the stories of brutality that they intervened and helped Cuba to win independence. Spain finally had to give up Puerto Rico, Guam and the Philippines to the United States as well.

Cuba soon became self-governing but was not completely independent.

The Caribbean

American business interests became very strong in the countries of Central and South America in the twentieth century, but these countries were politically rather unstable and had frequent riots and rebellions. American soldiers were sent into these countries to protect American lives and property whenever the United States government thought this was necessary. This led to the growth of anti-American feeling in these countries. This was particularly so in Cuba, where Fidel Castro led a pro-Communist revolution in 1956 and cut off relations with the United States. Castro became very friendly with Russia and even allowed her to build missile bases there. In 1962 President Kennedy managed to stop the Russians from supplying these bases.

Twentieth Century Presidents

Woodrow Wilson

When the First World War started in Europe in 1914, President Woodrow Wilson was very anxious to keep the United States out of the war, although most Americans sympathised with the British and French and Russians against the Germans and Austrians. The Germans began to use submarines to attack ships coming from America to Britain bringing supplies which Britain bought or borrowed from the United States. The United States government was angry because so many of her ships were attacked by German

Cuba's army on the march

Havana, the capital of Cuba

The sinking of the Lusitania *in 1915*

submarines and in 1917 she declared war on Germany. During the last year of the war, American soldiers fought together with the French and British to defeat the Germans and Austrians. Before the fighting was over, President Wilson tried to make a peace settlement. His suggestions were in the form of Fourteen Points and Wilson's proclamations encouraged the Germans to stop fighting in November 1918. They hoped that the Fourteen Points would be the basis for a just peace treaty, though when the treaty was drawn up it was much more harsh than the Germans had expected.

This was the Treaty of Versailles of 1919 and it also included a plan for setting up the League of Nations, an association which would discuss future world problems in the hope of settling them peacefully. But President Wilson was disappointed to find that, although the Europeans accepted his plan to form a League of Nations, his own country decided that they no longer wanted to be involved in European affairs. During the next twenty years before the next world war, the United States lent a great deal of money to countries in Europe which had suffered in the war, especially to Germany, but she did not take part in any political or diplomatic affairs.

Roosevelt and the Second World War

In 1929 the United States went through a terrible financial crisis. Many banks and factories closed and several million people were unemployed. This is called the Great Depression and it affected not only the United States but many countries all over the world as well. Franklin Delano Roosevelt was elected president in 1933 when the Depression was at its worst, but he soon gave the people new hope by his courage and enthusiasm. He made speeches in public and on the radio and did his best to get banks and factories working again and to provide state employment for the unemployed. New roads, dams and irrigation projects were started so that people had work to do. Roosevelt was personally a very courageous man. He had become paralysed when he was thirty-nine years old, but struggled to be able to walk again. For the rest of his life he had to use sticks and, later, a wheel-chair. Roosevelt was very popular and was re-elected three times. When the Second World War started in 1939 Roosevelt tried to keep his country out of this war, but American interests in the Far East soon became endangered by Japanese expansion, as we shall see in

Chapter 11. In 1941 the Japanese attacked the American naval base at Pearl Harbour in Hawaii and the United States entered the Second World War fighting on the same side as Britain and Russia against Germany and Japan. This time Americans fought both in Europe and in the Far East until Germany and Japan were defeated. Roosevelt died before the war ended, and it was his successor, Truman, who decided to drop two atomic bombs on Japan to force her surrender. These were the largest and most destructive bombs ever used in war and they completely destroyed the Japanese towns of Hiroshima and Nagasaki.

The United Nations

At the end of the war the United States took part in setting up another international organisation, the United Nations, which was a successor to the League of Nations. This time the United States did not refuse to be involved. In fact she offered land for the United Nations building in the middle of New York. Here the nations of the world have discussed their problems and disputes; they have tried to work together to prevent poverty, starvation and disease and to improve the economic conditions of the member countries.

Kennedy

The youngest president ever to be elected was John F. Kennedy, who became president in 1961 and was tragically assassinated in 1963. When he made his inaugural speech he said, 'Ask not what your country can do for you — ask what you can do for your country.' He inspired Americans with new hope of dealing with problems at home and abroad. At home he tried to get new laws passed by Congress to make sure that the negroes had full civil rights as citizens, that they could vote in elections, go to the same schools and universities as white people and use all the same shops, transport and hotels and other facilities. He encouraged young American men and women to give up one year of their life to go abroad, as members of the Peace Corps, to developing countries in

The statue of Liberty in New York

J.F. Kennedy is sworn in as President in 1961

Africa and the Far East to help work for the people of that country in whatever way they could. When he died, people all over the world felt shock and a sense of loss, because a very great man had died before he had finished his work.

Things To Do

1 Make a scrapbook about the United States including a map to show the boundaries.

2 Make a time chart of American History from 1783 to the present day.

3 Look up the most famous presidents in an encyclopaedia and make up a speech for each of them.

4 Imagine
  a that you are crossing America to look for gold in California. Describe your experiences.
  b that you live in the United States in 1861 and have to decide on which side to fight in the Civil War. Explain your decision.

5 Collect as much information about present day America as you can find in newspapers and magazines and make a list of the most important problems facing the United States today.

8
Africa

Africa – the 'Dark Continent'

Africa has often been described as the 'Dark Continent' because relatively little used to be known about it. It was a mystery to the outside world, partly because communication was difficult. There are great stretches of barren desert or dense tropical rain forest.

The native peoples of Africa did not develop a written language until recently. Our knowledge of ancient Africa comes mainly from the findings of archaeologists and from traditions passed from father to son. Such traditions are rather unreliable and archaeology gives rather an incomplete picture. Much of the building and art of Africa was in wood, and wood does not survive well for archaeological study. Many modern governments in Africa do not yet have the money to spend on large archaeological projects, and some are unwilling to do so.

In spite of this, archaeologists have unearthed evidence of the rich cultures of the peoples of old Africa. For example, important remains of a culture called Nok have been found in northern Nigeria. The people

African sculpture

Egyptian ships

who lived in this area from 800 B.C. to A.D. 200 were largely still in the Stone Age but they knew how to use iron and tin. They also made very striking figures in terracotta.

In Africa, however, change and growth came very slowly. This was due to the difficulty in communication. The tribes living in Africa found it difficult to share their good ideas with each other. Changes took place faster at the fringes of the continent, especially the northern fringes.

Early Contacts

Ancient Egypt was part of Africa, but the Egyptians knew little about the rest of Africa. They were curious about the vast unknown land. For a long time, gold, ivory and slaves reached Egypt from the upper stretches of the Nile River. From 3000 B.C. Egyptians were sending expeditions farther and farther south into the land inhabited by the Nubians. The Egyptians also sent naval expeditions through the Red Sea to visit places on the eastern coast of Africa, carrying back exotic goods and animals. The elephant came from Africa.

The Phoenicians built the city of Carthage in North Africa. In time, Carthage grew to be an empire in its own right. It controlled the trade in the western Mediterranean. It profited from the silver and tin mined in Spain and England, and from the caravan trade across the Sahara. The nomadic tribes of the Sahara brought ivory and gold from the south.

Carthage's position also gave it control over the important straits of Gibraltar, then called the Pillars of Hercules. The Phoenicians of Carthage were explorers too. Records show that, around 450 B.C., a Carthaginian called Hanno led an expedition down the western coast of Africa. He meant to build more colonies. He is said to have taken sixty ships and almost 30000 colonists. On this journey he met 'women with shaggy bodies, called gorillas' and saw a volcano which he called a 'mountain of fire'. After sailing as far south as the equator, he was forced to turn back as his supplies were running out.

Later the Greeks and the Romans explored other parts of Africa. Coins have been found as far south as Zanzibar off the coast of East Africa. The Romans conquered Egypt, the kingdom of Kush and a vast stretch of desert, as well as the Carthaginian Empire. There is also evidence to show that Arabs, traders from the East Indies, and Chinese sailors visited the east coast about 1 500 to 2 000 years ago. Asian plants, such as the banana and sugar cane, were probably introduced into Africa by some of these visitors. In very early times, African slaves, ivory and perfumes made their appearance in China.

African Empires

In the seventh century A.D. Arab invaders moved into Egypt and from there to North Africa. From Africa they swept into Spain. The invaders went because they wanted to preach their new found faith, Islam, to unbelievers. At first the Africans did not easily accept the new faith. There was fierce fighting, especially between the Berbers of North Africa and the Arabs, but the Arabs gradually managed to convert the Africans.

The Arabs brought Islam not only as a religion but also as a way of life. The Islam language, Arabic, became the first written language many Africans had. The Arabian horse was introduced into Africa at about this time, and revolutionised warfare. Camels too were brought in. This made travelling in desert regions easier. All these factors made possible the growth of great African empires south of the Sahara, in the grassland belt known as the Sudan. The earliest of these empires was Ghana which means 'war chief'.

Ghana was close to the edge of the Sahara between the upper Niger and Senegal rivers. Long before the coming of the Muslims, Ghana had become an important centre of trade. Moroccan goods and salt from the Sahara were carried in caravans to Ghana. They then took back gold and slaves. Neither the gold nor the slaves came from Ghana itself, but from the forest regions to the south. They did not use money but exchanged goods by bartering. The trade was

The modern capital of Ghana, Accra

destroyed in the early thirteenth century. No ruler after that was strong enough to revive the empire. In 1957 the state of Ghana in West Africa was named after the ancient empire, although it is almost 1 000 miles from its old site.

After the downfall of Ghana, another trading centre grew into an empire in a similar way. This was Mali, lying to the east of Ghana, on the river Niger. Mali prospered from the north-south caravan trade. In the fourteenth century, it had a great negro king called Mansa Musa. He was a Muslim and decided to make a grand pilgrimage to Mecca in 1324. He used this opportunity to show the North African countries how rich and

so important that Ghana became the main supplier of gold to mediaeval Europe. It was called 'Guinea gold', and inspired later Portuguese explorers.

For about seven hundred years the empire of Ghana dominated the western Sudan. When the empire was at its peak it had more than 200 000 soldiers. But Ghana's wealth attracted her ambitious neighbours. In the eleventh century a group of Muslim Berbers from the north invaded Ghana. They were fanatical religious reformers and they also wanted to control the gold trade. In 1076 they succeeded in conquering Ghana but could not hold it for long. Ghana regained its independence shortly afterwards but was

Timbuktu

Tribal chiefs in Ghana today

powerful Mali was. As a result, the great expedition became the talk of the region for many centuries. The caravan included five hundred slaves marching in procession, each carrying a long staff of gold. There were one hundred camels, numerous horses and fifty thousand ounces of gold. He spent so much gold in Cairo that an Egyptian official of the time complained that it lowered the value of the precious metal for twelve years.

The great pilgrimage was not just for show. Mansa Musa brought back with him a group of some of the best brains in the Muslim world to help improve his country. Among them were architects and engineers as well as poets and scholars. Colleges sprang up in Timbuktu, the chief city of Mali. Thanks to the efforts of Mansa Musa, Timbuktu in time became one of the most famous centres of learning. It rivalled, if not surpassed, some of the most famous European universities of the same period. Mali was strongly Muslim from the beginning, whereas Ghana only became Muslim at a later stage. Ibn-battuta, a fourteenth-century Arab traveller who visited Mali, wrote: 'They are careful in observing the hours of prayer, and assiduous in attending them in congregations, and in bringing up the children to them. . . . I visited (a friend), in his house on the day of the festival. His children were chained up, so I said to him, "Won't you let them go?" He replied, "Not until they learn the Koran by heart." '

Under Mansa Musa, the empire of Mali extended almost a thousand miles in the Sudan. When asked in Egypt how big his empire was, he answered that it took a year to travel from end to end. After the death of Mansa Musa, the empire broke up into a number of smaller kingdoms. Songhay was the most powerful. At the end of the sixteenth century, Moroccan invaders with guns conquered the Sudan kingdoms. The modern republic of Mali has the same name as the old empire.

As the powerful influence of Islam swept through a large part of Africa, a kingdom called Axum, in the mountains south of the Nile, resisted the new influence and kept its old religion and ways of life. Axum was in the region now called Ethiopia. The official religion of Axum was Christianity. Because of this Axum has been called an 'island of Christianity in a sea of Islam'. Legend has it that the people of Axum came originally from the region of Sheba in Arabia and were descended from Solomon and the Queen of Sheba.

Axum grew rich from the trade between Egypt and East Africa. Cattle and iron ore were exchanged for gold from the south. At first the people of Axum traded with the Arabs too, but when the Arabs became Muslims the relationship changed. Religious differences were strong and the Arabs were jealous of Axum's wealth. By the eighteenth

century they had cut off Axum from the outside world. The people of Axum were forced to retreat into the highlands and were isolated for several centuries.

The Coming of the Europeans

The introduction of iron was the first great influence which changed the lives of a large number of Africans; Islam was the second; the third great influence was the arrival of Europeans, who brought even greater changes. The first European explorations were in China and India. But in the fourteenth century trade with the east was blocked by the Muslims, so European nations began to explore and map the coast of Africa, to find an alternative route to India and the Spice Islands. They were also keen to find where the fabulous 'Guinea gold' and African ivory came from.

Portugal was the first country to send naval expeditions to explore the African coast. Prince Henry the Navigator was the moving spirit behind this venture. He set up a sea-school to train sailors for long voyages. Training and encouragement was indeed needed. Not only was the voyage full of danger, but many superstitions had to be overcome. Most people believed that the sea boiled near the equator and that the end of the ocean was a straight edge over which ships would drop and disappear for ever. In 1488 Bartholomew Diaz sailed round the Cape of Good Hope. In 1497 Vasco da Gama reached India by going further round Africa. The sea route to the East was at last open. For Europe and for Africa a new age had begun.

The Slave Trade

Soon after Vasco da Gama's voyage, trading stations were established at many points on the African coast. At first the Portuguese traded mainly in spices, gold and ivory. Gradually another source of great wealth became even more important. This was the trade in human beings — slaves. As early as the fifteenth century, African slaves were sold in Lisbon. Then because of the quick development of tropical plantations, particularly the new sugar plantations in Brazil, cheap labour was in great demand. Taking slaves to Portugal or Spain and then to Brazil took too much time and was costly. In the early sixteenth century, slaves began to be transported direct from West Africa across the Atlantic to South America, and later to North America.

The trade in slaves was much more profitable than traditional trade. Few Europeans actually had to go inland to capture the Africans. Instead they visited coastal stations where the local rulers handed over slaves they had either captured themselves or purchased in exchange for European goods, such as iron, copper, cloth, guns and ammunition. They did not use coins, but in time they worked out rough rules for exchange. Slaves were worth so many lengths of copper wire, so many guns or so many barrels of gun-powder. Slaves were often captured in war and because the trade was so profitable, it set tribe against tribe in unceasing slave raids. A rival chief or a slaver would set fire to a village by night and then

Henry the Navigator

Vasco da Gama

catch the villagers when they ran out. The Arabs were the chief slave catchers. Captured slaves would then be chained and marched down to the coast in human caravans. Some slaves changed many masters before reaching the coast. Not only the Portuguese and Spaniards were involved. In time traders from England, France, Denmark, Prussia and other European countries were active in the trade, as well as North Americans.

The treatment of slaves when they arrived at the coast was even harsher than the slave raids and the long marches. They were first stripped and examined carefully by ship doctors. Then they were branded on the chest with a hot iron and forced into the lower decks of the slave ships. As space was precious, they were packed so tightly that it was difficult to move. Those who became ill were simply tossed overboard. Others died in sea battles with rival slave traders or pirates. It has been worked out that only four out of every five slaves made the journey alive.

Arab slavers

The extreme inhumanity of the trade at last stirred the consciences of many European religious and political leaders. They forced their governments to stop the trade. In 1807 Britain stopped British ships from trading in slaves. The United States of America stopped Americans taking part in 1809. The delegates to the Congress of Vienna in 1815 all agreed to ban the trade. Generally speaking the slave trade had stopped by the early nineteenth century, but not before 8 000 000 slaves had been sold in the Americas alone.

Sierra Leone and Liberia

The slave trade had been officially stopped, but illegal trading continued. The British and American navies patrolled the African coast. But what were they to do with slaves taken from illegal traders? Britain and the United States solved this problem by founding the settlements of Sierra Leone and Liberia on the west African coast. Sierra Leone was founded in 1787 for freed slaves from England where they had been taken by retired colonists. They were later joined by negro veterans of the American War of Independence who had fought on the side of

Plan of a ship packed with slaves

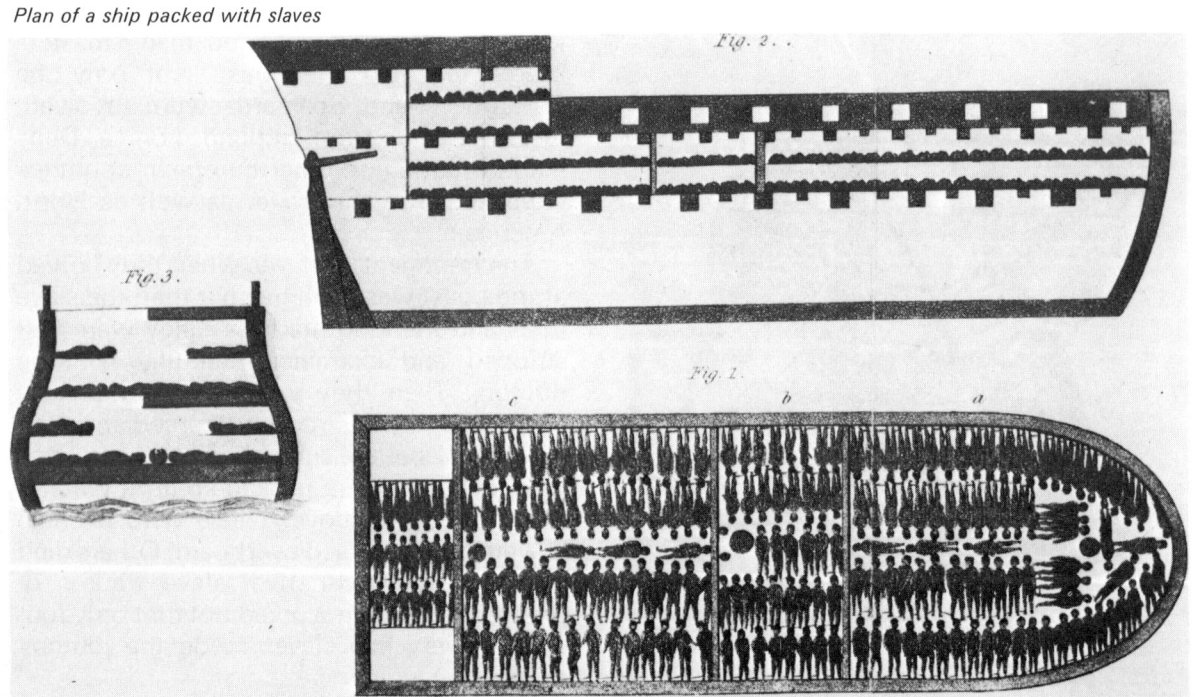

the British and who had escaped to Nova Scotia. Life on the settlement was hard at first. It was on the point of collapse when former slaves, freed from illegal slavers, joined the settlement. The population of the colony reached 40 000 in 1850. The town of Freetown was built and became the 'melting pot' of African and other cultures. Sierra Leone became independent in 1961.

Liberia was founded more or less in the same way by private American citizens for freed negro slaves early in the nineteenth century. About 12 000 moved there. The settlement chose the lone star as their flag and 'The love of liberty brought us here' as their motto. In 1847 Liberia became an independent state.

Modern Explorers

Although merchants of many European nations traded with Africa, they usually only set up trading stations on the fringes. Few penetrated into the interior. They had good reasons to keep away. The land was often difficult to pass. There were thick rain forests, rocky highlands or treacherous rivers. There were also hostile African tribes who were suspicious of outsiders, and tropical diseases to which Europeans had little resistance. Malaria was chief among them. They did not then know that a certain kind of mosquito carries this disease. They thought it was caused by hot damp air rising up from tropical swamps. The word malaria comes from Italian and literally means 'bad air'. It was not until the middle of the nineteenth century that quinine, an extract from a tree bark, was used in the treatment of the disease. The heart of Africa used to be called 'the white man's grave'.

The mystery of the African interior attracted a number of European explorers from the late eighteenth century onwards. They were hardy men, prepared to take the risks. Some succeeded: others perished. The modern explorers of Africa were of three types. Firstly, there were those who explored either to satisfy their own desire for adventure or for academic interest. Secondly, there were the missionary explorers who wanted to bring Christianity and various

Natives receiving Dr Livingstone

improvements to the lives of the African people. David Livingstone was the best known. Thirdly, there were those like Henry Stanley who explored Africa to find out about the possibilities of making money.

David Livingstone

David Livingstone was born in Scotland of rather poor parents in 1813. His father was a tea salesman. At the age of ten, he began working in a cotton mill but he was a very ambitious boy. After work, he studied Greek, theology and medicine and eventually qualified as a doctor. He then joined the London Missionary Society and wanted to go to China. War had broken out in China at that time so he was sent to Africa instead.

He left England in 1840 and spent the next sixteen years in Africa exploring mainly southern Africa. His main interest was river systems. He reasoned that the rivers provided a good means of communication. They would help in opening up the interior of Africa to the outside world. He discovered a magnificent waterfall on the Zambezi River. This he named the Victoria Falls. His travels were recorded in his popular book *Missionary Travels and Researches in South Africa.*

His book was read by influential people in the government. He was sent out again in 1858 at the head of an expedition which explored eastern and central Africa. During this second journey, Livingstone explored the area around Lake Nyasa. The death of his wife made him cut short his stay. He returned in 1862 to write *The Narrative of an Expedition to the Zambezi and its Tributaries.* It was during this journey that Livingstone saw with his own eyes many slavers still actively at work. He felt that the only way of stopping this was to open the area to outside influence.

When he was invited to go out to Africa again in 1865, he gladly accepted. This was to be his last journey. He found even more evidence of slave trading. He wrote that he saw a group of Arab slavers suddenly beginning to shoot at the women in a crowded market place. Hundreds were killed. He thought he was 'in hell'. Things began to go wrong shortly after he set out. His helpers all ran away. One of them even disappeared with his valuable medicine box, including his supply of quinine. Heavy rains, sickness and Arab slavers delayed him. For several years, no one was quite sure where Livingstone was. Then in 1871 Henry Stanley 'found' him, ill and tired, on the shores of Lake Tanganyika, at a town called Ujiji. Livingstone heard about the opening of the Suez Canal in 1869 from Stanley. He refused to go back to England. With fresh supplies brought by Stanley, he continued to explore and was found dead one morning two years later, kneeling in prayer beside his bed.

Livingstone spent thirty years exploring Africa. He travelled over one third of the continent. The records of his travels were eagerly read, and influenced countless people all over the world. His efforts to combat slavery made many governments pass stricter laws against it. His last journey was recorded in *The Last Journals of David Livingstone in Central Africa.*

Henry Stanley

Henry Stanley is best known for two things: he found David Livingstone and he opened up the Congo region. Stanley was born in Wales. He was an illegitimate child and as a result had an unhappy childhood. He spent some years in a charity home. He found life there so unbearable that he ran away at

The opening of the Suez Canal

fifteen to become a cabin boy on a steamer bound for America. There he was adopted by Henry Morton Stanley who gave him his name. After Mr Stanley's death, young Stanley fought in the American Civil War and later became a sailor and then a journalist. He found his last job most satisfying.

When he was working for the *New York Herald,* his editor asked him to go and find Livingstone. Reports of the famous explorer's earlier journeys were eagerly followed. Readers all over the world were concerned about his sudden disappearance. Stanley's paper guessed that finding Livingstone could be one of the biggest 'scoops' of the century. Stanley set out in 1869 by way of Egypt, covering the opening of the Suez Canal on his way. In 1871 he finally located Livingstone in Ujiji. He was so moved on meeting the aged missionary that he could only say 'Dr Livingstone, I presume.'

When Livingstone died, Stanley was ready to step into his place as Africa's best known explorer. Supported by influential newspapers, he set up an expedition in 1874 to trace the course of the mighty Congo River. He followed the course of the river to the sea, but it was a dangerous journey. He fought over thirty battles, often against great odds. Several of his white assistants died. He was harsh with his men but his never-say-die determination won him their admiration.

Stanley was disappointed when he could not interest the British government in developing the Congo. He saw great opportunities for trade and profit in the area. Shortly afterwards, he found an eager patron. King Leopold II of Belgium had been following Stanley's travels with keen interest. He had always dreamed of building an empire in Africa. Leopold persuaded Stanley to return to the Congo in 1879. Stanley spent five years there. He built a road and over forty stations along the river, into which he put a number of steamers. He also made treaties in the name of Leopold with local chiefs. He began the trade in rubber and ivory with the natives. His energy and his firmness earned him the nickname of Bula Mutari, or 'Rock Smasher'. Stanley had helped in the creation of the Congo Free State which stretched over an area of 1 000 000 square miles south of the Congo and which was the personal property of Leopold II.

The British in Africa

The 'Scramble for Africa'

The establishment of the Congo Free State entirely changed the nature of European activities in Africa. Instead of just trading at the fringes, European nations were now actually taking over large pieces of land. Once the race began, there was no return. No nation wanted a rival to have more colonies. In a way the 'scramble' was also started by Bismarck, the Chancellor of Germany, who thought expansion in Africa would make the nations forget their quarrels in Europe. The scramble was also helped by such pioneer empire-builders as Cecil Rhodes who gave his name to Rhodesia. Although he did not officially represent Britain, Rhodes' dream was to extend the empire from Cairo to Capetown. He grew fabulously rich on the gold and diamond mines. He helped Britain to take up large territories in southern Africa using his money and influence. By the end of the nineteenth century, nearly the whole of Africa was under European control. The most notable exception was Ethiopia, but even that country was soon to be invaded by Italy.

The Twentieth Century

At about the turn of the century, several important changes occurred. In the Congo Free State, Leopold's rule created great hardship for the Africans. They were forced to present a fixed amount of rubber. Anyone

Henry Stanley with a servant

Boers returning from hunting

who failed to do so was often punished by having a limb cut off. Slavery was also practised on some plantations. Leopold claimed that he was not aware of the atrocities, but the international outcry was such that the Belgian government decided in 1908 to take it away from the personal control of Leopold. The Congo Free State then became known as the Belgian Congo.

The next major change followed the First World War. Germany was defeated and was no longer allowed to keep her African colonies. These were divided among the victors by the League of Nations as mandated territories. Then came the Second World War. Many Africans fought in the war. After the war, the Africans were sure that they could rule their countries as well as Europeans if they had the education and the determination. Modern education in Africa, as well as overseas study, enabled many Africans to gain experience as government administrators or politicians. They now wanted to be free from European control.

The former colonies and protectorates gained independence one by one. In some cases, independence came peacefully. In others, independence came with confusion, violence or bloodshed. Many white people had come to think of Africa as their home. In some of the new states, the races lived peacefully with each other. In others there were serious racial problems, especially in South Africa. In South Africa and Rhodesia the white minorities continue to control the government. By 1970, nearly all countries in Africa had become independent. The major exceptions were the Portuguese territories of Angola and Mozambique.

Africa before 1914

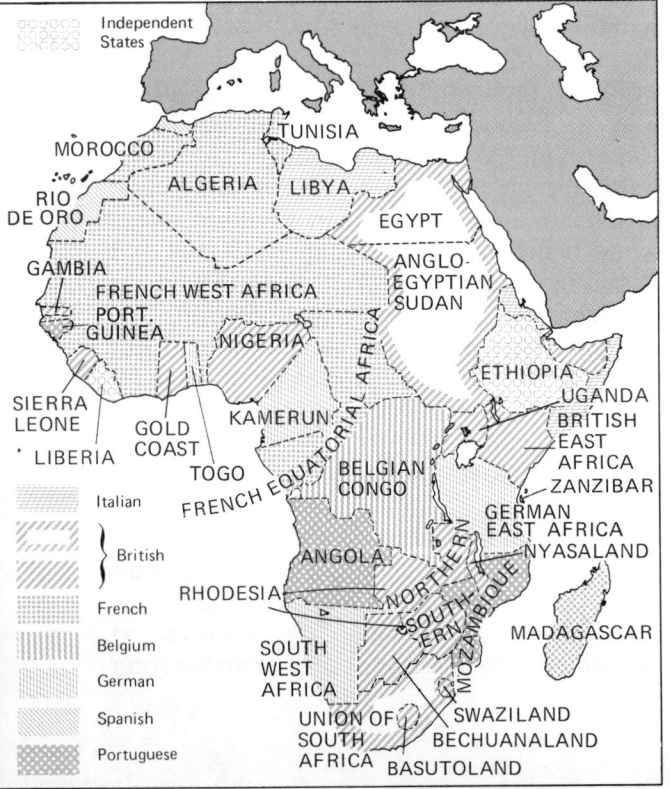

Present-day Africa

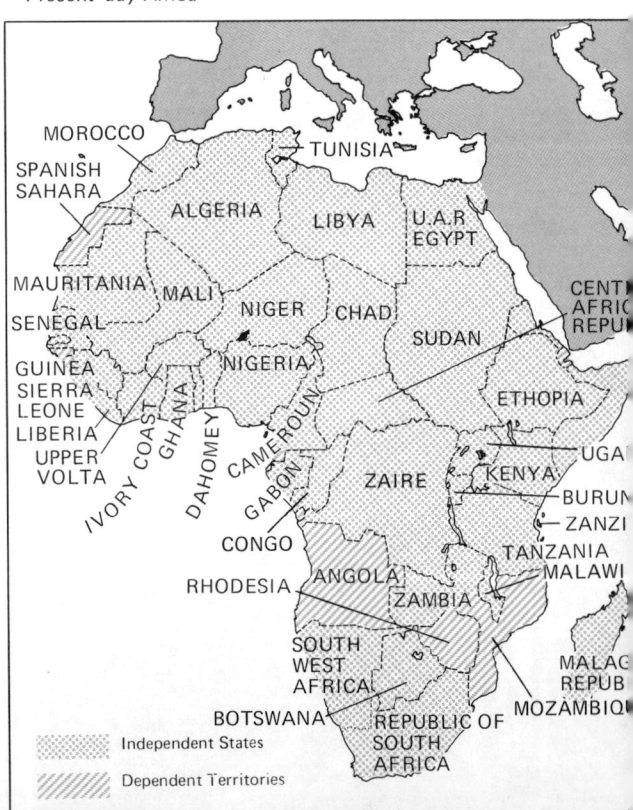

Things To Do

1 Why was Africa, at one time, called the 'Dark Continent', and why has it been especially difficult to unearth evidence of the history of ancient Africa?

2 Why did the city of Timbuktu become important in the fourteenth century?

3 What were the causes and effects of the African slave trade, and why did it officially come to an end in 1815?

4 Trace Livingstone's and Stanley's journeys on a map of Africa. Imagine that you were accompanying one of them and describe your experiences.

5 Write an account of the life of Cecil Rhodes.

6 Find out which African states have become independent during the twentieth century. Describe the difficulties they have faced and the progress they have made. Each project group could concentrate on one particular state.

9
South-East Asia

The Spice Trade

We read in Chapter 1 about Marco Polo and the stories of the East that he brought back to Europe. Merchants especially were encouraged to make the long journey overland to bring back the silks, damasks, jewels and spices they found there. Spices were very important, for the Europeans had no way of preserving food at that time. They could salt the meat to stop it going bad, but then it tasted most unpleasant — spices could disguise the taste of bad or salty meat and so were very popular. Merchants could therefore get a very high price for them.

Spices came from the islands in South-east Asia. The journey overland became more and more dangerous during the fifteenth century because the Turks were always attacking travellers; so Spanish and Portuguese navigators decided they must find a sea route to the East. Columbus was the first to try but he discovered the West Indies instead. The Portuguese, however, succeeded when Vasco de Gama sailed round the Cape of Good Hope at the end of the century. Soon Spanish, Dutch, British and French merchants made the journey and set up trading posts in South-east Asia.

They faced fierce competition from the Arabs, because they had traded there for many years. The Arabs sold their spices to merchants in Venice and from there they were sent to other parts of Europe. But the Europeans eventually controlled the spice trade themselves. As so often happens in history, trade was the cause of empire building.

Trading Posts

The most important of the Portuguese trading posts were Goa in India, Malacca on the west coast of the Malay Peninsula, and Macao on the coast of south China. All these trading posts were established in the sixteenth century. During the seventeenth century the Dutch drove the Portuguese out of Malacca, and established more trading posts for themselves in the Indonesian Islands which were known as the Spice Islands. The English also tried to set up trading posts in the Spice Islands, but the Dutch drove them out and gradually took over control of all the islands; these were then known as the Dutch East Indies.

The Philippines

The Chinese sailor Cheng Ho, whom we read about in Chapter 1, came to the Philippines at the beginning of the fifteenth century. The Philippines became a Chinese colony, but when Cheng Ho's voyages were

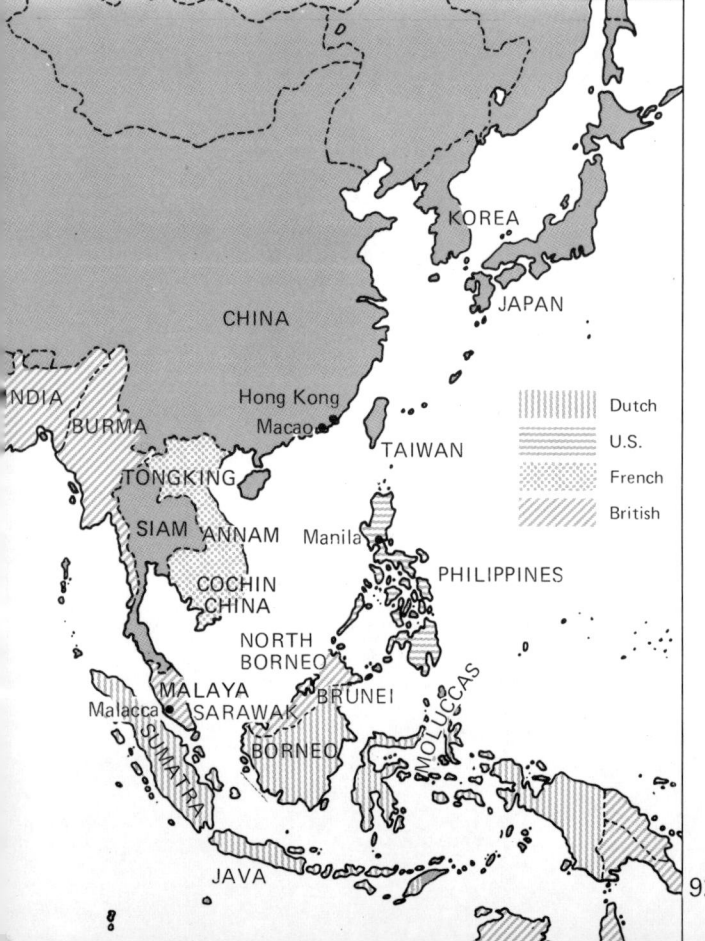

South-east Asia in the early twentieth century

Macao

stopped the Chinese abandoned the Islands.

The Spaniards then discovered the islands in 1521 when Magellan landed there. The straits of Magellan are named after him. The history of the Spanish in the Philippines is connected with their activities in South America. The Spaniards conquered Mexico in 1521 and so could easily get to the Philippines from there. They founded a colony. Missionary priests converted the people to Christianity and found they readily accepted the new faith and the Spanish culture and civilisation. Spanish became the official language. The Philippines remained closely connected with the Spanish colonies in South America. When these broke away in the nineteenth century, it was difficult for the Spanish to retain control of the Philippines. They could not get there so easily and so the colony was isolated.

When the Americans fought Spain over Cuba in 1898, an American fleet destroyed a Spanish fleet in Manila Bay and the Philippines were granted to the United States at the Peace Treaty ending the Spanish-American War. The United States ruled the Philippines until 1946.

Thailand

During the period of European expansion in South-east Asia, Thailand, which was then known as Siam, was the strongest country. This kingdom had to fight frequent wars with the Burmese, the Khmers of Cambodia and the Vietnamese of Annam and Tongking.

But it kept its strong position until the nineteenth century. Two remarkable kings of this period are worth noting, Mongkut 1851–68 and his son, Chulalongkorn, 1868–1910. Both kings had studied western languages and knowledge and wanted to modernise the kingdom and keep on good terms with western countries. Mongkut signed friendship treaties with Britain, the United States and other countries in Europe.

King Mongkut

The central office of the Dutch East Indies in Bengal

In this way he opened up the country to foreign trade and influences. Mongkut encouraged developments in science and technology. One of his interests, astronomy, was his downfall. He arranged for all his court and many guests to visit a place where there was to be an eclipse of the sun, but unfortunately the place was very unhealthy, and the king caught a fever and died. As Chulalongkorn was then only sixteen he decided to travel for five years before he took over full power. On his return from his travels he introduced many reforms. His descendants have continued to rule Thailand up to modern times. However, the monarchy is now constitutional and the king no longer has the same authority as before.

Burma

Thailand's most serious rival in South-east Asia was Burma, which overthrew Thai rule for brief periods in the sixteenth and eighteenth centuries. Burma's longest period of peace was under the Toungoo dynasty which ruled from 1605 to 1752. During this time Burma shut out foreign contact rather like the Tokugawa shoguns in Japan. Travellers visited the country, but trade did not become important until the beginning of the nineteenth century. The British East India Company had been trading successfully in India and wanted to extend its con-

trol to Burma. So Britain found reasons to invade Burma three times during the nineteenth century. In 1885 Britain conquered the country. But there was much resistance because Britain treated Burma as another province of the Indian Empire. Burma had quite different customs and religious ideas and naturally resented this treatment. It took five years for Britain to establish law and order. After the Second World War, Burma became independent.

The French in Indo-China

French influence in Indo-China began in the seventeenth century when missionaries came to make converts in this area. French influence gradually became strong enough for France to take over Annam and Tongking. These two states had been under Chinese influence for several hundred years and did not welcome foreign influence. However, French troops were stronger than theirs and so they had little difficulty in gaining control.

Cambodia

Soon France was able to extend her control to neighbouring Cambodia. Cambodia accepted French influence more readily because the people wanted protection from the Thais. The Thais were threatening to invade Cambodia. The French developed the area economically and introduced French language and customs. The education system was the same as in France and the more intelligent students were sent to French universities.

France granted full independence to Cambodia in 1954 under King Sihanouk. In 1955, however, he abdicated in order to lead his own political party and took the title, Prince Sihanouk. He kept his country peaceful, and introduced some economic reforms. He followed a neutral foreign policy and ruled quite strictly. He did not allow much opposition and finally a group of army officers seized power while he was out of the country in 1970. Cambodia then became involved in the troubles of the neighbouring South Vietnam.

Vietnam

At the beginning of the twentieth century there were Nationalist risings in Tongking and Annam. A Nationalist party was formed and, in 1931, it grew into the Indo-Chinese Communist party. Its leader was Ho Chi Minh. He set up a republic in Tongking, but war started between Tongking and the French which lasted until 1954 when the French withdrew after a terrible defeat at Dien Bien Phu. A major conference of world powers was held at Geneva to discuss the problem of Indo-China. Vietnam was divided into North and South, and Cambodia and Laos were confirmed as independent states. However, Communist groups in South Vietnam soon started to attack the rulers and were supported from North Vietnam. The United States entered the war to help South Vietnam in its attempt to stop Communism from spreading any further in Indo-China.

The British in Malaya

The Straits Settlements

Penang was the first British foothold in Malaya. It was founded by Captain Light in 1786 and became a prosperous trading post. Britain's next opportunity for expansion in this area came during the Napoleonic Wars. The Dutch were involved at home with Napoléon's invasion of their country and were not able to defend their possessions in the Dutch East Indies. Britain took these over and although she had to hand them back after the wars, she did gain Malacca as a permanent base. Another British acquisition was Singapore which Sir Stamford Raffles founded. This was by far the best harbour for trade. The three cities, Penang, Malacca

Ho Chi Minh

Sir Stamford Raffles

and Singapore became colonies and were known as the Straits Settlements. A British governor was appointed to look after British interests in this area.

The governor found that trade was made difficult because of the disorders in the Malay peninsula. The states were always at war with one another and the time was ripe for a strong power to step in and take control. The governor of the Straits Settlements took action and persuaded the Malay states to accept British advice on all matters except religion and customs. In this way Britain brought law and order to Malaya. Prosperity increased when the tin mines were put into order. Chinese workers came to work there and they controlled the mines. The British brought rubber trees over from Brazil and this too grew into a major industry. Indians came to work on the rubber plantations.

The British also came to control areas in Borneo. James Brooke, a British subject, helped the Sultan of Brunei to control the rebels in his territory. The Sultan was so

Rajah Brooke

grateful for his help, and for later services, that he made James Brooke his successor. The Sultan had no children; so the rule of the white Rajahs of Sarawak began. Britain also developed a protectorate over the small state of Brunei.

Nationalism and Independence

We will interrupt the story of Britain in Malaya to look at the general situation in South-east Asia at the turn of the century. In 1900 the European powers controlled large areas of South-east Asia and their power seemed to be very strong. However, within fifty years, almost every part of the region had achieved independence. There were several reasons for this development.

Many students had been sent from South-east Asia to study in the universities of Europe. There they learned about democratic systems of government and about Socialism and Communism. While studying abroad they lost contact with their own customs, and returned home determined to change their homeland. Revolution seemed, to many, the only way to challenge the rule of the colonial powers, and thus revolutionary independence movements grew up every-where.

Japan provided an example of a country which had adopted western ideas and reforms so successfully that she defeated not only China but also Russia. Japan had modernised her government and army and navy so well that she could compete with, and even defeat, a western power. We shall read about Japan in Chapter 11.

The First World War weakened the colonial powers and encouraged the politically active peoples of South-east Asia to demand reform and independence. The attitudes of the colonial powers varied. The Dutch had no intention of making any changes which might damage trade with the Dutch East Indies. The French hoped to extend their cultural influence so that the people of Indo-China would not want to be independent of France. Educated men in the French colonies could rise to high positions either in their own countries or in France, and there was a lot of inter-marriage which helped to strengthen bonds. The British wanted to develop representative government and educate the people so that power could be transferred when the people were politically ready, but there were usually problems of race or language which they tried to solve before independence.

The Japanese Invasion

In 1941 and 1942 Japan invaded and took over all the colonial empires of the powers in South-east Asia and set up the Greater East Asia Co-Prosperity Sphere. This was intended to be a series of independent states under the influence of Japan. In fact Japanese military rule was severe and there were food shortages in many places. At first the Nationalist leaders of South-east Asia were impressed by the speed with which the Japanese had conquered the region and believed that the Japanese would win the whole war, so they co-operated with them hoping to get the best future solution. When they realised that eventually the Americans would defeat the Japanese in South-east Asia, the National-ists realised that they must set up independent states quickly before the colonial powers were able to return.

Indonesia

In Indonesia which was once owned by the Dutch, Dr Sukarno, the leader of the Indo-nesian independence movement, had co-operated with the Japanese during the war. When the Japanese realised that they would be defeated, they helped Sukarno to declare the independence of Indonesia. Sukarno set up a republic in 1945 and started to govern the country. For the next four years, the Dutch tried to re-establish control. Finally a United Nations commission persuaded the Dutch to accept the new republic. Dr Sukarno continued to govern the country as prime minister for many years and gave the country great political and international importance. But his plans were expensive and destructive to the country's economy. His successor, General Suharto, has tried to

improve the industry and trade of the country and bring it back to prosperity.

Malaysia after the War

During the Japanese occupation, resistance had been led by the Chinese Communist group in Malaya and supported by most other Chinese living there, for there had been terrible persecution of the Chinese by the Japanese. After the war Britain tried to find a satisfactory plan for the independence of Malaya which would give political inde-pendence to all the people living there — Malays, Chinese, and Indians — but the problem was a difficult and complicated one. When the Malays seemed to be getting more power, the extreme Communist Chinese group started guerrilla activities against the British, attacking people, blowing up rail-

President Sukarno

Tengku Abdul Rahman on Independence Day

Lee Kuan Yew

ways and roads and retreating into the jungle where they could not be easily pursued. This continued for twelve years and was known as 'The Emergency'. The independence of Malaya was proclaimed in 1957. Malaya became a Federal State and each Sultan retained power in his own state, while taking part in a Federal Council. Each Sultan in turn took the position as king or Yang di Pertuan Agong. The first king was Tengku Abdul Rahman. He guided the nation wisely for many years, first as king and, later, as Prime Minister of an elected Parliament. In 1963 Sarawak and Sabah in Borneo were joined with Malaya to form Malaysia. Malay was the national language and Malays continued to have preference in the state over the Chinese and Indians. Singapore, however, had a mainly Chinese community and her interests seemed to be very different from Malaysia. She therefore left the Federation and became an independent republic in 1965 under her Prime Minister, Lee Kuan Yew. Singapore has continued to be a very prosperous trading community.

Macao

Macao has remained a Portuguese colony long after all the other Portuguese colonies in South-east Asia were lost, but its importance has diminished because the Pearl River brings down so much mud that it is difficult to keep the habour open for modern steamers. It has had to depend on shipping heavy goods through Hong Kong, thirty miles away across the Pearl River mouth. Macao also has no airport. Tourism is an important income earner; there are also light industries.

Hong Kong

When the British acquired Hong Kong from China in 1841 as a trading post on the China coast, no one expected that it would grow to a position of such commercial importance. At that time it was inhabited by a small fishing population and by pirates. Hong Kong has an excellent natural harbour and is in a very good position in relation to the rest of South-east Asia. British merchants were quick to realise that it would be an important base for trade with China and they started to use Hong Kong for ships carrying opium. Hong Kong became especially important during the Opium Wars of 1839–42 which are dealt with in Chapter 10. Hong Kong Island and, later, Kowloon Peninsula, was granted to Britain for ever as a result of these wars. After the wars many Chinese came to live and work in Hong Kong because the job prospects were good, and it was peaceful and well governed. Trade was allowed to develop freely without restrictive tariffs. More and more mainlanders came to live in Hong Kong, especially during periods of political unrest. During the Second World War, China and Britain became allies against the invading Japanese. Hong Kong fell on Christmas Day, 1941, and was under occupation for four years. After the war, Hong Kong has surpassed its previous prosperity and absorbed thousands of mainlanders who fled when civil war erupted. From an entrepôt, Hong Kong has become an industrial centre. However, prosperity has brought with it many new problems. Chief among these are an increasing crime rate and a lack of housing and education facilities.

Things To Do

1 Why was the Spice Trade so important?

2 Find out about the following people and make brief biographical notes:
King Mongkut   Captain Light
Stamford Raffles Dr Sukarno
Ho Chi Minh   Lee Kuan Yew
Tengku Abdul Rahman

3 Make two large maps to show the world in 1900 and the world today. Use flags or markers to show the colonial empires, and the nations which became independent in the twentieth century.

4 Write a paragraph explaining the growth of Nationalism in South-east Asia during the twentieth century.

5 Make a drawing of James Brooke as the white Rajah of Sarawak.

6 Write a short essay about Western influence in Hong Kong. You could illustrate it with newspaper cuttings.

7 Try to find out what the main religions are of each of the states discussed in this chapter.

10
Modern China

The Manchus

The Manchus were a group of tribes living mainly in the area in north-eastern China known as Manchuria. They were descended from the tribe which founded the Chin dynasty in the twelfth century. The Manchus were driven north of the Great Wall by the Mongols when they founded the Yüan dynasty.

The Manchus were not the only inhabitants in Manchuria. Many Chinese also settled there, especially in the south in the area called Liaotung (遼東) to the east of the Liao River. Liaotung consists of fertile plains and good harbours and was not much more than two days' sailing distance from Shantung province. In fact Liaotung was ruled as part of Shantung. The Manchus therefore came into close contact with the Chinese and learnt their ways and customs. The Ming emperors did not rule the Manchus directly. Instead, local chieftains were recognised as rulers as long as they remained loyal to the Ming Empire. They were expected to present tribute to the government and in turn the emperor rewarded them with honours and titles. When a ruler became disobedient, the emperor would punish him by sending him on a military expedition north. On more than one occasion, the Koreans joined forces with the Ming because they too were anxious to keep the peace in that region. The Ming emperors felt safe as long as the narrow pass to the north-east of Peking, called Shanhaikuan (山海關) or Mountain and Sea Pass, was in Chinese hands. This narrow strip of land, with the mountains and Great Wall on one side and the sea on the other, held the key to Manchuria. A strong garrison guarded this important pass at all times.

Nurhachi (努爾哈赤)

The Manchu tribes became a powerful force

Nurhachi

under Nurhachi's leadership, their tribal hero, just as the Mongols had been united by Genghis Khan. Nurhachi's grandfather was a tribal chieftain. Both his grandfather and his father were killed by Ming forces when they were betrayed by a rival Manchu leader. Nurhachi was then twenty-five. He vowed to avenge their deaths. Gathering together a small band of close followers, he spent several years tracking down his enemy. The Ming garrison did not interfere with their fight and in fact refused to grant refuge to the hunted man. In the end Nurhachi captured and killed his enemy and took over his possessions. From these Nurhachi extended his control over the lands held by lesser chieftains and emerged as the most powerful Manchu leader. The Ming Empire was forced to recognise his position. The Ming emperor followed the practice of letting the Manchus rule themselves, and granted him the title of the 'Dragon-tiger General' (龍虎將軍).

The Manchus were united into a powerful force under Nurhachi's leadership. He employed a number of Chinese advisers. He erected a strong castle to house his government. He also obtained an important source of money when he took control of the profitable trade in ginseng, a valuable herbal medicine, which was used in China as a general tonic. The Chinese thought that the ginseng found growing wild in the forest and mountains of Manchuria was of the highest quality. In addition Nurhachi traded in furs and horses.

Nurhachi himself spoke Chinese very well and enjoyed reading Chinese novels. But he thought the Manchus should have a written language of their own. They spoke Manchu, but had never written it down. So although Mongolian was at first the official language, Nurhachi ordered experts to borrow the alphabet from the Mongols so that writings could appear in Manchu. In this way Chinese ideas were translated into Manchu. The Chinese style of government was borrowed too and Chinese scholars served in it. The government was no longer tribal, with the older citizens in the highest positions, but was based on ability. Men with talent achieved responsible jobs without regard to race or birth. Many Chinese found working in the Manchu government a rewarding career.

Nurhachi's main strength, however, was in the army. He used the system of 'banners' to combine military and civil control. The area under Manchu rule was divided into districts. Each had a different coloured banner. The banner district was taxed as a single unit and had to supply a fixed number of armed soldiers. At first there were only four banners, but the number soon increased to eight and then twenty-four, including Chinese and Mongol banner districts. The banner system made the whole Manchu nation into a big armed camp, ready to move and fight at short notice.

By 1616 Nurhachi felt that the Manchus were strong enough to overthrow the Ming emperor. He proclaimed himself the emperor of the Chin dynasty which is known to historians as the Later Chin (後金) dynasty. Two years later he occupied part of Liaotung and then established his capital at Mukden (Shen-yang 瀋陽).

The Conquest of China

When Nurhachi died in 1626 two very able successors continued his policies. Abahai (皇太極), Nurhachi's fourth son, drew up the plans for the conquest of China. In 1636 Abahai proclaimed himself Emperor of the Ch'ing or Pure dynasty at Mukden. When he died, his son succeeded him as Emperor but, as he was only a young boy of six, his uncle, Dorgon (多爾袞), ruled for him. He ruled for seven years before returning power to the Emperor. Dorgon completed the conquest of China.

The Manchus prepared for the conquest of China first by extending control over areas north of the Great Wall. They then invaded Korea and forced the country to accept Manchu rule. They sent expeditions to subdue the areas in the north and the west. The Manchus made raids into China to capture labourers and livestock and to test Chinese defences.

Fighting the Manchus was a strain on the Ming, but its fall was due more to internal weakness than to outside pressure. Power was completely in the hands of the royal princes and rich landlords. The peasants were starving, so they welcomed the rebel leader, Li Tzu-ch'eng (李自成), and there

The rise of the Manchus

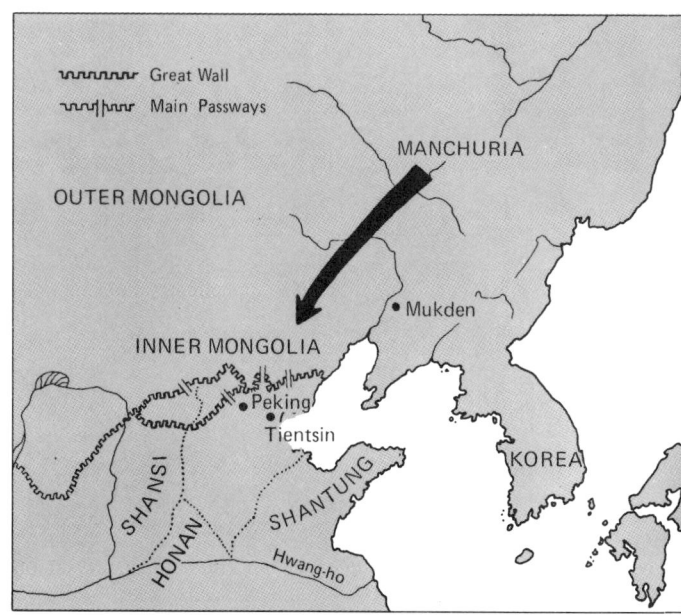

A battle between the Manchus and the Ming

were many risings. Finally the peasants marched with Li to Peking. They were so powerful that they captured Peking. The Ming emperor, hearing the news, committed suicide and sent his three sons into hiding.

But Li's triumph was short. One of the Ming generals was so alarmed by the power of the peasant army that he decided to call in the help of the Manchus. Manchu troops won back Peking and killed Li. They also killed all the Ming family so that the way was open for them to take control of Peking themselves. The general who called in their help probably did not mean this to happen.

The Manchus had not yet conquered China completely. Chinese resistance was still strong in the south. One of the most colourful figures in the resistance movement was the son of a pirate who operated on the China Sea from Macao to Japan. The Dutch who traded there called him Koxinga (國姓爺) as he was allowed to use the family name of the imperial house. He controlled a large part of the coastal region opposite Taiwan Island. In 1661 Koxinga landed on Taiwan and drove the Dutch away from the island. Using Taiwan as his base he continued to make raids on the mainland. The Manchus did not have a strong naval force, so it was difficult to control him. They banned foreign trade, and moved the population away from the coastal region. Neither of these methods was very successful. When Koxinga died, his successors still carried on in the name of the Ming court. Finally the Manchus succeeded in occupying Taiwan with some help from the Dutch in 1683. This was during the reign of K'ang-hsi.

K'ang-hsi (康熙)

K'ang-hsi was the greatest ruler of the Ch'ing (清) dynasty. He was probably as great as Louis XIV of France and Peter the Great of Russia. He was fond of outdoor life and was a skilled huntsman. He was a good scholar and an excellent administrator. His reign was extremely long: it lasted from 1661 to 1722. K'ang-hsi laid a firm foundation for Ch'ing rule in China. His main achievements were winning the support of the scholar class, the suppression of resistance and the extension of the frontier.

Although the Manchus established themselves in Peking, they did not have complete control of the country. Their quick progress so far had been due partly to the successful use of Chinese methods and partly to the strength of the banner forces. But people did not like Manchu rule. This could be seen in the continued resistance of the Chinese south of the Yangtze. Most of the scholar class refused to work with their new rulers, because they still looked upon themselves as Ming subjects. Some sought refuge in the mountains. Some actively supported groups of armed rebels. A few simply starved themselves to death. At least one fled to Japan and was honoured by the Tokugawa shogunate. The majority adopted a wait-and-see attitude. K'ang-hsi tried to show them that he was a patron of scholarship. As proof he sponsored the ambitious project of compiling the history of the Ming dynasty. It was common practice in China for a new dynasty to compile a standard history of the previous one, so K'ang-hsi cleverly used this as a means of gathering the best scholars of the time into his service. A special selection test was held. About two hundred top scholars were invited. Forty did not come. Out of those who came, he chose fifty. Most of these were from parts of China where resistance was strongest. The chosen scholars were given high ranks in the government. K'ang-hsi also commissioned other literary works. The well-known K'ang-hsi Dictionary is still used today as a standard reference. The complete works of the Sung scholar, Chu Hsi (朱熹), were published. A great encyclopaedia of 5 000 volumes was compiled as well as a selected summary on painting and calligraphy. These measures succeeded, and K'ang-hsi won the support of the scholar class. In a country which valued learning this was even more effective support than a strong army.

The Chinese court painted on a porcelain plate

103

The success of this policy was shown when K'ang-hsi faced the revolt of the three feudatories (三藩). When the Manchus first occupied China, the three Chinese generals who had helped them were given almost complete control over large areas in south and south-western China as a reward. These were called feudatories. They had been given a great measure of autonomy and the Ch'ing decided they could no longer allow so much freedom. The Ch'ing were strong enough now to force the feudatories to reduce their power. However, the feudatories rose up in rebellion. A civil war followed. The remaining resistance forces based in Taiwan joined in. For a time the Manchus were in danger of losing the whole of China south of the Yangtze. But, soon, the leaders of the revolt quarrelled among themselves. After eight years of fighting, the rebels were finally defeated in 1681.

K'ang-hsi was equally concerned about the frontier. He personally led an army into Mongolia to subdue the Mongols. Ch'ing control was extended deep into Inner Asia. When Mongol tribes were involved in troubles in Tibet, his army brought the whole of the region under the firm control of the empire.

Yung-cheng (雍正)

K'ang-hsi had over thirty sons of whom twenty survived childhood. When K'ang-hsi died in 1722 there was a struggle for the throne and his fourth son, Yung-cheng, managed to seize power. He had obvious ability, but was suspicious of the people that surrounded him. Several of his brothers were put into prison and died there. Others were robbed of any real political or military power. The activities of imperial princes were carefully supervised. Spies were employed to watch for any sign of disobedience and to do secret duties for him. Many stories were told about the deeds of these dreaded agents.

Yung-cheng's reign was short compared with the one before and the one after him. His main achievement was the strengthening of the government organisation. The highest level in the civil service had been the Grand Secretariat, but the officials there were appointed usually because they were senior rather than because they were able. Yung-cheng felt that this was unsatisfactory. He created a new body of five or six senior officials called the Grand Council (軍機處). The Council consisted of the Emperor's most trusted advisers. Its members met the Emperor at dawn every day. Important decisions were made quickly and with the least fuss. The Grand Secretariat still existed, but it mainly handled routine matters. The creation of the Grand Council gave the government much greater efficiency. It also enabled the government to respond to any emergency with greater speed and more freedom from set rules.

Ch'ien-lung (乾隆)

Yung-cheng left the throne to his son, Ch'ien-lung in 1737. Ch'ien-lung admired his grandfather more than his father and tried to be like him. He was active in outdoor life and was a good scholar and painter.

Unlike K'ang-hsi, he was fond of show and glory. During his reign Chinese armies were sent to fight in Inner Asia, Burma, Tibet, Nepal and other nearby areas. He was proud of these battles and they later became known as the Ten Great Campaigns (十全武功). The frontier of the Ch'ing empire was at its greatest extent during his reign. It was also the greatest in Chinese history except when it was under the Yuan dynasty of the Mongols.

Ch'ien-lung's campaigns did not benefit the Empire greatly and they were also extremely costly. In his later years, Ch'ien-lung lost his sharpness of judgement. He allowed corrupt officials who pleased him to take important positions in his government. They, in turn, encouraged corruption of lesser officials throughout the Empire. The most notorious of these, when at last caught by the succeeding emperor, had collected the incredible personal fortune of nine hundred million taels of silver. Among the items confiscated were a pure jade horse measuring nearly one metre high, 14 300 bolts of silk, and almost five hundred mechanical clocks imported from Europe.

Shanghai

Chinese dish of the reign of
Ch'ien-lung showing a spring
festival

The Portuguese arriving in Japan

A Japanese No play

Ch'ien-lung

When Ch'ien-lung retired in 1795 the Ch'ing dynasty had passed the peak of its power. The costly wars and the widespread corruption were the main causes of decline. In 1795 a large-scale uprising took place in the mid-western regions. This was led by a secret anti-Manchu organisation known as the White Lotus Society (白蓮敎). It took about ten years for the Ch'ing Empire to suppress the rebellion.

Jesuits in China

Jesuits had been coming to China ever since Matteo Ricci opened the way for Roman Catholic priests during late Ming times. K'ang-hsi was a man who would listen to others; he was friendly with the Jesuits and accepted their assistance in many fields. Jesuits taught his officials about western methods of studying astronomy and helped to make corrections in the calendar. They also gave advice on the drawing of maps and in dealings with other Europeans, especially the Russians. Their knowledge of mathematics, science, music and painting made them welcome at court, but the number of people they actually had contact with was small. There were few Christians. Those who were converted wanted to keep some of their ancient Chinese customs, but the missionaries could not agree on whether this should be allowed.

Fewer Jesuits came to China in the second half of the eighteenth century. So although Ch'ien-lung still allowed them to stay, their strength gradually grew weak. The Jesuits had been successful in influencing those in power, but, generally speaking, they left only a small mark on Chinese history. There were very few converts from the working people. But the reports they made on China were eagerly read in Europe and helped to increase European interest in China.

British Merchants in China

Merchants in Europe were also anxious to come to China to trade. The country was so big that it made an ideal market for European goods. Chinese goods also found a ready market in Europe. Products like tea, silk and porcelain fetched good profits in many parts of the western world.

We read in Chapter 9 about the interests of the Europeans in South-east Asia; British traders had more interest in China than did other Europeans.

At first, British merchants traded with India and later with China. The British East India Company was given the sole right of trading in India and all areas east of India. By the end of the eighteenth century, the Company was keeping an agency called a 'factory' in Canton. The main article of trade in the East used to be spices, but, by the eighteenth century, tea had replaced spices. Tea-drinking had become a popular habit in England. Figures state that every Englishman drank two pounds of tea per year. The China tea trade became so important that the

The emperor of China receiving British envoys

A Canton 'factory'

English government relied on tea taxes for one-tenth of its total income at the end of the eighteenth century.

On the other hand China did not want to buy very much from England. Fancy goods like mechanical clocks, watches and music boxes only paid for a small part of the tea. Silver paid for most of it, particularly silver gained in trading with India. The emperor granted the merchants the use of Canton as a trading port only as a favour. Strict regulations were set to control the trade in Canton. In time these regulations and practices came to be known as the 'Canton System'.

British merchants were dissatisfied with the Canton System. They tried very hard to put the trading relations on a firm and agreed basis and to obtain permission to increase the volume of trade. The British merchants persuaded their government to establish contact with the Chinese government. As a result two diplomatic missions, the Macartney mission of 1793 and the

Amherst mission of 1816, were sent to China, but these failed to change the existing conditions.

The Opium Wars

The situation changed when the English found that there was a new commodity they could sell in China – opium. British ships brought opium from India to China and charged a high price for it. The Ch'ing government was alarmed at the cost and the emperor forbade the sale of opium. However, official corruption was so common and widespread that it was available in large quantities in Canton. Some farmers in India grew opium specially for the Chinese market. With the immense profits made from the sale of opium, the merchants could now pay for the tea.

Finally, the emperor decided to put a stop to the opium trade. He sent a special commissioner to Canton to do this. This man seized a cargo of 20000 chests of opium and tipped them into the sea at Canton. Britain, outraged, declared war.

This was the first of the Opium Wars and lasted from 1839 to 1842. British forces showed clearly that European weapons, training and methods of war were far superior to Chinese methods. China was forced to accept defeat and to sign the Treaty of Nanking of 1842. She had to pay for the opium which had been destroyed. Five ports were opened to British trade and Hong Kong Island was ceded to Britain. Other privileges concerning British consuls and tariff rates were also granted. Soon other foreign powers followed the British example. They requested and were given similar treaties.

The Treaty of Nanking did not settle all problems. British merchants in time felt that the treaty did not go far enough. The Chinese thought that too much had been given away. In 1857 war started again when a dispute over a British ship arose. France joined the war because a French missionary had been killed. The war is known as the Second Opium War. It ended again in defeat for the Ch'ing government. The Treaty of Tientsin in 1858 and the Convention of Peking in 1860 gave further privileges to Britain and France. Other powers obtained similar treaties.

A battle during the Opium Wars

The Taipings

The Taiping Rebellion

The repeated defeat in war with foreign countries was just one indication of the general decline of the Ch'ing government. Signs of this general decline could be seen in the late Ch'ien-lung period. The corruption of officials, the rapid increase of the population and the frequent occurrence of natural disasters all played their part in arousing the discontent of the people. As in the past, uprisings among hungry peasants were common during hard times. Added to this now was the hatred felt towards the Manchus by the Chinese. The secret societies became active again.

Around 1840, a scholar who was known as Hung Hsiu-ch'üan (洪秀全) of Canton organised a secret society called the God Worshippers' Society. Hung was a baptised Christian and he had learnt much from the missionaries. His society believed in the importance of the Ten Commandments. There was a very strict code of rules for good behaviour. Many bad customs of the past were discarded, such as the unfair treatment of women.

In 1850, Hung Hsiu-ch'üan led an armed rebellion. Province after province fell to the advancing rebels. The Ch'ing army had become so weak that it could only trail behind. Hung Hsiu-ch'üan then occupied the city of Nanking and made it his capital. He called it T'ai-p'ing t'ien-kuo (太平天國) which means Heavenly Kingdom of Great Peace. He was known as the Heavenly King (天王) and his capital as the Heavenly Capital (天京). His followers were called Taipings.

After many months of fighting without success, the Ch'ing government was forced to rely on the help of Chinese leaders, especially the scholar-general Tseng Kuo-fan (曾國藩). He formed a new army from the militia forces. Gradually this army proved to be a match for the Taipings. When internal quarrelling developed among the Taiping leaders, Tseng's forces were more successful. In 1864 Nanking was beseiged. When news came that the city had fallen, Hung took his own life. With the death of the Heavenly King, the movement collapsed. The Taipings were strong for fifteen years and overran sixteen provinces. Millions of lives were lost in the fighting. It was the worst civil war in Chinese history.

After the Taiping rebellion the Ch'ing government tried to strengthen itself with help from leaders who had risen during the civil war. Some officials were very impressed by the power of western weapons and western science. They wished to find out more about them. So they sent students overseas to study. As a result the Chinese built arsenals and factories and laid railways and a telegraph line. A new army and a new navy were created and trained under foreign advisers. Officials of the old tradition were suspicious of all these new measures. Their champion was Empress Tz'u-hsi. She exercised great influence behind the throne. The new 'Self-strengthening Movement' was therefore not allowed to go very far.

China went to war with Japan over Korea in 1894 and the new navy and the new army met their first test; however, the Japanese defeated them. China signed the Treaty of Shimonoseki in 1895 giving Japan control over Korea. The dramatic defeat of the new Chinese sea and land forces marked the failure of the self-strengthening efforts.

Tz'u-hsi (慈禧)

When the young Emperor Kuang-hsü (光緒) tried to introduce some basic reforms in the government in 1898, Tz'u-hsi again took the side of the conservatives. The reform programme collapsed after one hundred days when Tz'u-hsi kept the Emperor a virtual prisoner in the imperial gardens. She next hunted down the Emperor's advisers. The main leaders managed to escape.

When a group of anti-foreign fanatics called the Boxers became active in the south and moved towards Peking, Tz'u-hsi encouraged their activities. They were called Boxers because their training included physical exercise. The Boxers attacked churches and foreigners. Then they attacked the legations and foreign missions in Peking. When foreign forces arrived in China to protect their subjects, Tz'u-hsi declared war on the foreign countries concerned. This enlarged the scale of the conflict. It led to the occupation of Peking by foreign troops and the flight of Tz'u-hsi and the court from the capital.

Tz'u-hsi

Peace was finally restored when the Boxer Protocol was signed in 1901. The Ch'ing government had reached a point where little improvement could be made. A new reform programme was announced but no notable effort was made to put it into practice. Meanwhile other revolutionary groups were planning not to reform the government, but to overthrow it.

Trial and execution of foreigners during the Boxer Rebellion

Chairman Mao at a rally

The Republic

In 1911 the revolutionary movement, led by Sun Yat-sen (孫逸仙), overthrew the Manchu government. A general of the old régime called Yüan Shih-k'ai (袁世凱) was made the first president of the Republic when he agreed to join the revolution.

The establishment of the Republic did not bring peace to China. On the one hand, the Japanese tried to gain more and more privileges in China; on the other hand, local generals called 'warlords' (軍閥) fought each other for power, with little regard to the central government at Peking. In this confusion, Sun Yat-sen established a rival government in Canton. He accepted the help of the new Russian republic, especially in the founding of a military academy at Whampoa, Canton. When Sun Yat-sen died his lieutenant, Chiang Kai-shek (蔣介石), took over. He organised a military campaign against the north. In the course of the campaign, a quarrel developed between Chiang Kai-shek's Nationalists and members of the new Chinese Communist Party.

The Civil War

With the return of peace, the old quarrels between the Nationalists and the Communists came into the open again. Civil war then followed and Communist forces won. In 1949 they drove the Nationalists out of the mainland. The People's Republic of China under the leadership of Mao Tse-tung (毛澤東) was proclaimed in Peking in the same year. The Nationalists took refuge in Taiwan and proclaimed the Republic of China.

Things To Do

1 How was Manchuria ruled by the Ming government? Was this a successful policy? Give your answer in a short paragraph.

2 Write a short essay on Nurhachi.

3 How did the Manchus conquer China? Give your answer in a few short paragraphs.

4 Ch'ien-lung tried to imitate his grandfather. Do you think he was successful? Answer briefly.

5 Write a short paragraph on the Taiping Rebellion.

6 Draw a portrait of Sun Yat-sen and then write a short biography of him.

7 Stage a class exhibition of the Second World War, including reports of interviews with witnesses. If possible arrange for the showing of films of the Second World War.

8 Write short notes on five of the following:

Liaotung	the 'banner' system
Yung-cheng	The Three Feudatories
Taiwan	Jesuits in China
tea	opium
Tz'u-hsi	the Civil War

11
Modern Japan

'Treaties with Five Nations'

On 8 July 1853, four 'black ships', two of them steam-powered, appeared out of the mist at Uraga Bay, a fishing village outside Edo. The Japanese fishermen working in the bay hurriedly drew in their nets and fled ashore 'like wild birds'.

Thus began a new era in the modern history of Japan. For over two centuries, the shoguns' government had enforced the policy of closing the country to any relations with western countries. Even shipwrecked sailors were sometimes treated harshly to discourage foreign ships from venturing too near Japan's shores. But this policy was unpopular with a number of western countries who wanted Japan to be open to the sale of their goods. Russia, the closest country, made the first attempt to persuade the shoguns' government to open the country to trade. As early as 1792, a Russian captain called Laxman tried to land at Hokkaido in the north but was told to go to Nagasaki instead. It was not until 1804 that he sailed to Nagasaki only to find the port firmly closed and the Japanese as suspicious as ever of foreigners. Then came the Americans. They saw Japan both as a promising market and as a country which could provide refuge and supplies for America's whaling ships and a depot for storing coal for the now increasingly more common steamers. The American government put Commodore Biddle in command of two ships to pay a friendly visit to Japan. He arrived in 1846 but was curtly told to leave.

The American government therefore decided to make a second more determined effort. Commodore Matthew Calbraith Perry was given a squadron of four ships and 560 men and the imposing title of 'Commander-in-Chief, US Naval Forces, East India, China and Japan Seas and Special Ambassador to Japan'. Perry, nicknamed by his friends 'Old Bruin' or 'Old Brown Bear', was a large and

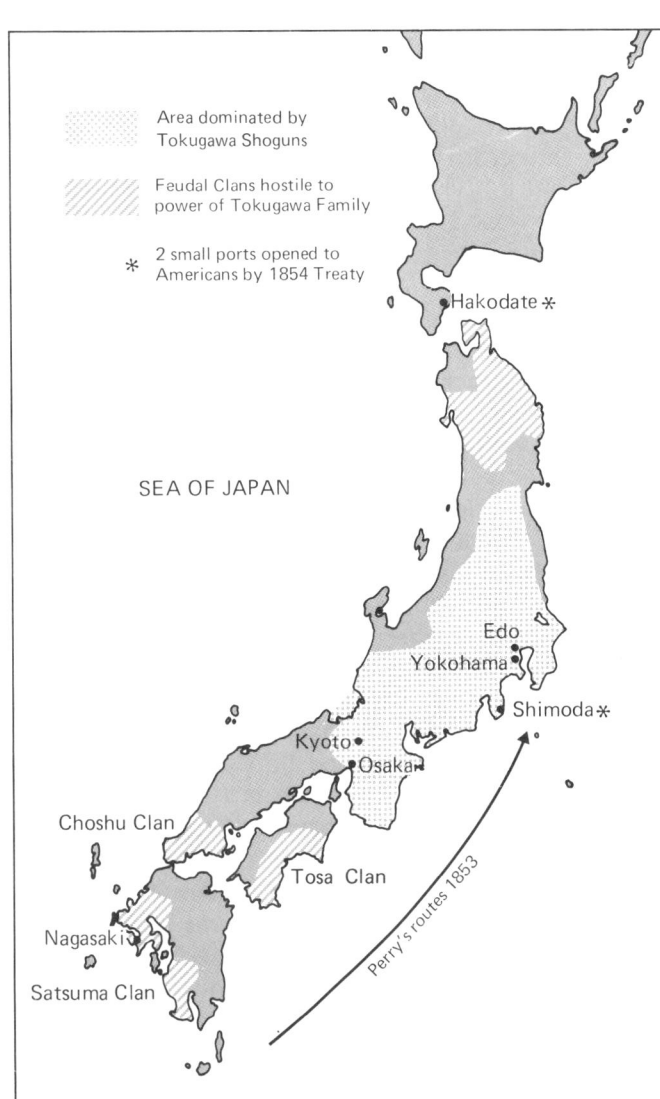

Japan in 1850

solemn-looking naval officer. When he arrived at Uraga Bay he refused to deal with anyone below the rank of governor of the province. When the meeting was finally arranged on shore, Perry had his ships alerted for battle while his hosts took the equally careful step of surrounding the conference with 5000 troops. Perry delivered to the governor a letter from President Fillmore which was addressed to the Japanese emperor. The tone of the letter was friendly but Perry's own message was very firm. He promised that he would return the following spring for an answer – 'with a much larger force'.

When Perry returned in February 1854, he was as good as his promise. He came with twice as many ships on which were 250 cannons. There were three steam frigates in his squadron which in strength made up twenty-five per cent of the whole United States navy. He insisted on holding the conference at Kanagawa, now part of Yokohama, because it was nearer Edo. The conference was conducted through an American interpreter who knew Dutch but not Japanese, and a Japanese interpreter who knew Dutch but not English. After several days of hard bargaining, during which Perry showed he would use force if necessary, a treaty of Amity and Friendship known as the Treaty of Kanagawa was signed. This opened two Japanese ports, Shimoda and Hakodate, to American shipping. An American consul was permitted to live in the former. Shipwrecked sailors were promised friendly treatment. Japan also agreed to grant to the United States without further bargaining any extra privileges given to other countries. This was known as most-favoured-nation treatment.

On this last visit, Perry brought along as gifts a small model steam railway engine, a telegraph set and one hundred gallons of whisky. He set the engine up on shore on a short length of track. His Japanese hosts were very impressed and enjoyed the ride on the roof of the miniature train. Perry also invited Japanese officials to tour his ships. They displayed great curiosity about almost everything on the ships. An eye-witness recorded:

'(They) peered into every nook and corner, peeping into the muzzles of guns, examining curiously the small arms, handling the ropes, measuring the boats, looking eagerly into the engine room and watching every movement of the engineers and workmen as they busily moved about the gigantic machinery of the steamers.'

There was no doubt that the Japanese were very interested in what western science and technology could do. Indeed, now that the new treaty forced them to open the country, they were only too eager to master these secrets of western power for themselves.

Following the American example, the British, the Russians and the Dutch all asked for the same treatment. As a result, similar treaties were signed with these countries. However, when the American consul Townsend Harris arrived to take up his residence in Shimoda as agreed, he found that he was not very welcome. Slowly he became friendly with his hosts and managed in 1858 to persuade the shoguns' government to sign a new treaty. The Harris Treaty, as it was

The Japanese inspecting a telegraph set

known, provided for the exchange of ministers, the opening of new ports, the fixing of taxes on imports at a moderate level and the right of American citizens accused of breaking the law to be tried by their own officials. As before, similar privileges were granted to the Dutch, Russians, British and French. These treaties are called by the Japanese 'Treaties with the Five Nations'.

The Cry of Son-No

The coming of the foreigner divided the nation into three camps. One group thought Japan should recognise the superiority of western culture and learn from it. Another thought limited trade would be a good thing economically. But the third group thought Japan should remain isolated and break agreements with the five nations. This was the opinion at Kyoto, where the emperor lived. Gradually the cry of 'Son-no Jo-i' or 'Honour the Emperor, Expel the Barbarians' became widely heard. In the ten years after the signing of the treaties, Kyoto grew in importance and Edo declined as a political centre of Japan.

The position of the emperor became increasingly important. He had strongly criticised the shogun for his weak foreign policy. Many provinces shared his opinion and were in favour of asking the shogun to 'restore' political power to the emperor. Chosu and Satsuma in the south-west were key provinces in bringing this about. They had never really accepted the rule of the Tokugawa shoguns who had taken advantage of their remoteness from Edo to strengthen their own forces on modern lines. The young samurai of Chosu and Satsuma were energetic and well educated. At first the two provinces wasted their time in fighting against each other, but in 1866 they came to a secret understanding and agreed to forget their differences. In January 1868 they seized control of Kyoto and announced an 'imperial restoration'. The decisive battle with the shoguns' forces was fought outside Kyoto. Thanks to able leadership and better training the provincial forces completely routed the shoguns' army after three days of

Foreign envoys at an imperial audience

fierce fighting. They then marched on to Edo where the shogun handed over the city without much resistance. The long unbroken reign of the Tokugawa shoguns, beginning in 1603, thus came to an end, and after seven centuries of rule by the shogunate, the emperor once more began to control his land.

The Meiji Era

The first aim of the slogan 'Son-no Jo-i' or 'Honour the Emperor, Expel the Barbarians', which was to bring about the downfall of the shogun's government, had now been achieved. But the leaders of the country were no longer anxious to carry out the second aim seriously. Bands of roving samurai had killed or bullied foreigners in Japan, and some provinces had fired on foreign vessels passing close to their coasts.

Nevertheless the new leaders realised that Japan was not yet strong enough to fight the western powers. Instead they decided to strengthen and modernise the country by borrowing foreign methods. When this was done, they believed that foreign powers would then look upon Japan as their equal. When Meiji became emperor in 1867 at the age of fifteen the country was still very unsettled. But by the time his long reign ended in 1912, Japan had more than realised her aim to make foreign powers regard her as an equal.

Japan becomes modern

One of the most important problems which faced the new leaders was the breakdown of effective government. The Tokugawa shoguns, especially the later ones, allowed the daimyo too much power in their own provinces. The system of holding their families hostage was so clumsy that it had to be given up in the early 1860s. Clearly, if Japan was to make herself strong, the central government must have the power to make its orders obeyed throughout the land. So, by stages, power was taken out of the hands of the local lords. As a first step Edo was renamed Tokyo, which means eastern capital, and made the seat of the imperial government. In 1871 all the provinces were given up to the central government. These were then divided into units called prefectures. The officials who ruled the prefectures were appointed by the central government which could now apply overall planning to the whole country.

Steps were also taken to create a strong modern army. The central government took over the local armies and merged them into an Imperial Army on the French model. The best trained core of the new army was called the Imperial Guard (Konoe). This was commanded by the famous Chosu leader, Yamagata, who also became Minister of the Army. The navy was built on the British model and was mainly controlled by Satsuma men. Service in the armed forces was made compulsory to all citizens. This broke the long tradition of samurai control of the country's armed forces.

Crowds bow before Emperor Meiji's car

A street scene in nineteenth-century Japan

116

Similarly remarkable reforms were made in the country's economic life. The government announced a new fixed tax on land in 1873. This was a three per cent tax on the value of the land and it replaced all the old ineffective ways of collecting revenue in the old days. The money collected was then used to support the government, to build up the armed forces and to start new industries. The government started many new industries and also encouraged rich merchants to use their money in the same way. The government also led the way in building railways, telegraph lines, shipping lines and banks.

The same reforming energy was given to the country's educational system. Bright young students went to Europe and America to study. Many of these became well-known national figures in later life. Foreign experts were also invited to come to Japan to teach specialist skills. As early as 1871 a system of compulsory six-year primary education was put into effect. Many famous Japanese universities, among them Tokyo University, Waseda University and Keio University,

were founded in this period.

Laws were also rewritten with the advice of foreign experts. As a result the treaty powers agreed to give up privileges in law for their citizens. The treaties were therefore now no longer regarded as 'unequal'.

The New Constitution

In April 1868, when the emperor had just been 'restored' to power, he made a famous promise to the country. This was known generally in English as the Charter Oath. It was drafted by a Chosu samurai. The articles were:

1 General meetings shall be called so that decisions can be made according to public opinion.
2 All classes shall rule the country together.
3 All classes of people shall be able to fulfil their ambitions.
4 Bad customs of the past shall give way to laws based on justice.
5 To strengthen the country, knowledge shall be sought from all over the world.

Women in Tokyo march to demand equal rights

The emperor announces the Meiji constitution

bership had to be drawn up in the form of a constitution. A leading Chosu statesman, Ito, led a study mission to Europe to find out which European constitution Japan could best borrow as a model. Several political parties also sprang up in the meantime to try to win as many seats in the coming elections as possible.

After much debate, the Meiji constitution was finally announced in 1889. It was based chiefly on the German constitution, and the main points were:

1 The emperor is the supreme ruler of the country.
2 A Parliament called the Diet shall be created.
3 The Diet will be made up of an upper section called the House of Peers and a lower section called the House of Representatives.
4 Seats in the House of Representatives will be filled by elections.

The actual elections were held early in 1890 and the Diet first sat in November of the same year. In spite of the constitution and the Diet, the small group of old leaders continued to be the real rulers of Japan for many more years. They acted as the emperor's personal advisers and came to be called the 'genro' (elderly leaders).

New Customs

Western influences brought tremendous changes to the Japanese way of life in the Meiji period. In learning western methods, the main aim of the Japanese people was to strengthen the country so that it could be looked upon as equal by the western powers. But they soon found it convenient to take over the western way of life entirely. Gas lighting and electricity became available in the last quarter of the century. Japan adopted the metric system of measurements. The western Gregorian calendar replaced the lunar calendar. The rickshaw, a kind of sedan chair on modern wheels, also became popular. Beef, which the Japanese did not much like, was now widely eaten. The western short hair-style replaced the old samurai top-knot for men. For ladies, Victorian style dresses and fancy-dress

Exactly what the emperor meant by the first article was not clear. Some leaders thought that the emperor intended to create something like a Parliament to rule the country. The seats of such a Parliament would be filled by national elections. As time passed, it became clear that this was not the intention of the emperor: important decisions continued to be made by the small group of leaders of not more than a hundred who had played an important part in the restoration of imperial rule.

As time went on more and more people demanded the calling of a Parliament. They strongly criticised the leaders ruling in the name of the emperor, saying that they were old and corrupt. At last the emperor had to promise that a Parliament would be called in 1890. Before that could be done a set of rules concerning its organisation and mem-

Modern Tokyo

dancing parties were considered very fashionable. New words came into the vocabulary. For instance, the morning coat became in Japanese 'moningu'.

The craze did not last. Before long the speed in copying western customs slowed down, but the fact remained that Japan's modernisation had fundamentally changed the country, even in the way the ordinary people lived.

Two Successful Foreign Wars

Ever since the first treaties were unwillingly signed with foreign powers, Japanese leaders believed that one of the aims of the reform programme was to build a modern army and a modern navy. This would enable Japan to follow a strong foreign policy and to be looked upon as 'equal' by the powers. Japan was especially interested in what was going on in the neighbouring country of Korea; even Hideyoshi had tried to conquer the country. So, when internal troubles appeared in Korea, Japanese leaders, especially those who had close connections with the army, wanted to use them as an excuse to intervene. But China also had close historical ties with Korea. She would not allow Korea to be controlled by Japan. When further trouble occurred, China and Japan could not agree on a common solution. War was therefore declared in 1894.

Within a few months, Japanese troops had seized Port Arthur and were prepared to invade Peking, the Chinese capital. China was forced to make peace, and Japan gained very important advantages by the Treaty of Shimonoseki of 1895. By defeating China, Japan showed the world how strong she had become.

The growing strength of Japan, however, became a major worry to Russia. She looked on Japan as a threat to her eastern borders. Indeed, Russia herself was thinking of obtaining some of the advantages Japan had gained. So, in 1896, together with France and Germany, Russia demanded that Japan should return some of the territories she had gained to China. Japan was forced to accept Russia's demands, but she did not forget this insult. In 1902 Japan signed an alliance of mutual assistance with Britain, the foremost sea-power of the day. This gave Japan much greater confidence. When the quarrel with Russia flared up again over Korea and Manchuria, Japan was now prepared to fight against Russia and war was declared in 1904. The decisive battle of the war was won by the Japanese fleet under Admiral Togo's able command in 1905. Virtually the whole Russian navy was destroyed. Peace was finally concluded by the signing of the Treaty of Portsmouth, in the United States of America, in the same year.

From Meiji to Taisho

In 1912 Emperor Meiji died at the age of fifty-nine, and his son Taisho succeeded him. Meiji's reign had been a long one, spanning nearly half a century. Those fifty years were the most significant in Japan's history, seeing her change from an isolated state into a strong modern power. The very name 'Meiji' means 'Enlightened Rule'. Nearly all the aims of the restoration leaders had been achieved. Japan had built up a modern, well-trained army and navy. She had also made important progress in education, in political organisation and in industrialisation. She had gained the respect of the powers by winning two major wars. The powers had abolished their earlier 'unequal' treaties. In 1912, therefore, Taisho inherited a country which seemed to have an even brighter future ahead, yet already there were signs of trouble. The original leaders were still alive, but they were tired old men. (Ito was assassinated in 1909, but Yamagata carried on until he died in 1922.) Younger men wanted to share some of the power so far kept by the small group. The armed forces became more and more difficult for the civilian government to control. The population also was expanding far more rapidly than the increase of wealth.

The First World War and Japan

Japan had been very successful in her wars with China and Russia. As a result she gained many advantages especially in South Manchuria and Korea. Korea became part of the Japanese Empire in 1910. Japanese leaders were encouraged by their successes and were ready to go even further. The chance came when the First World War started in 1914.

Japan was bound by her treaty with Britain to join with the Allies against Germany. It was in any case in Japan's interest to do so because it gave her a chance to establish supremacy in areas that were threatened by Germany. Japan started by taking over the province of Shantung in China which had been under German domination. Then, taking advantage of China's weakness, Japan issued a document known as the Twenty-One Demands, which seriously threatened China's independence. There was widespread criticism at home and abroad, but as the Europeans were involved in a war of their own they were not in a position to interfere and so China had to agree to many of the demands. Western powers were very worried over growing Japanese ambitions.

In 1917 the Bolshevik Revolution took place in Russia. Again Japan took advantage of the confusion by invading Siberia. Her excuse for doing so was that the Czech soldiers in Russia who were caught in the middle of the revolution needed help. At first Britain and America agreed until they discovered that Japan was sending many times more troops than was necessary. At the end of the war Japanese troops stayed on although other allied troops had left. They did not leave until 1922 when the cost of keeping the troops there became too big and the criticism against Japan's action had become severe.

Compared with her allies, Japan's actual fighting involvement was small during the war, but her gains were great. She took over the German possessions in China and in the Pacific. Above all, her industries made great gains because many countries which used to buy European goods had to buy now from Japan, as European countries were more busy fighting than producing goods for sale. In 1921 the powers met in Washington to settle a number of outstanding problems in the Far East: Japan had to agree to give up the former German possessions in China and the Anglo-Japanese Alliance was discontinued. These decisions meant a setback for Japanese foreign policy.

The Rise of the Militarists

The first few years of the Taisho Period were golden years for Japan, but towards the end of the reign Japan faced a series of troubles. The Taisho Emperor suffered from ill-health and was so sick after about 1920 that his son the Crown Prince had to do most of his work.

In 1918 widespread rioting broke out in many big cities all over the country. The cause was the sharp rise in the price of rice, the main food of the people. Then in the autumn of 1923 a terrible earthquake shook the whole Tokyo-Yokohama area. Within two minutes two-thirds of Tokyo and the whole of Yokohama had been destroyed. Altogether 107 000 people died. In 1926 the Showa Emperor took over, but his reign also began badly. In the same year about forty small banks closed through bankruptcy. This made the many small merchants who did business with the banks suffer, and many people lost their life-savings. Generally, people blamed the hardship on the big merchant firms usually called the *zaibatsu*, or 'money groups' and on corrupt politicians. From 1929 to 1930 a period of very poor business hit the United States and this had its effect throughout the world. These years are sometimes called the Great Depression. Japanese farmers now found that no one could afford to buy the silk they made and many farmers were ruined.

The army had always distrusted the politicians and the big businessmen. As soldiers came mainly from farming families they were personally affected by all these troubles. The army tried to seize power from the politicians and to persuade the government to follow a strong foreign policy.

In 1931 a conflict arose between the Japanese army stationed in southern Manchuria, known as the Kwantung Army, and the inhabitants. It gave an excuse for the army to occupy a large part of the area. The Japanese government was not even told about this until later and then they had to accept what had happened. This set a very poor example. From then secret societies, encouraged by the army, carried out a great number of plots and assassinations. Politicians who did not agree with their views simply were killed. In 1936, in a bold attempt, 1 500 men from the Tokyo garrison killed three government ministers in one single day. Although the plot did not go much further, it showed how powerful the army was.

From 1936 the government was controlled by army generals. They, and the politicians who supported them, were called militarists. Immediately plans were made to broaden the area of fighting in China. In the following year Japanese forces invaded China. Already the militarists in Japan were talking of creating a 'new order' made up of countries in Asia controlled by Japan.

Japan's Empire in 1914

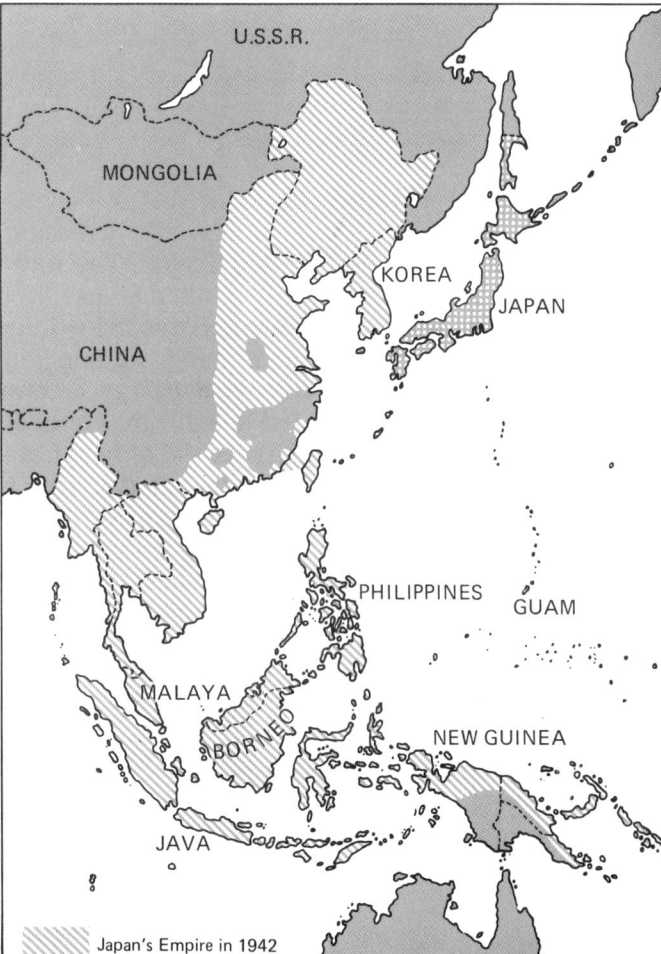

121

Destruction scene in Hiroshima

The Japanese sign the surrender document

Tora!

Japan's war policy met with increasing criticism from the United States. The navy did not wish to fight the United States in a sea war, but the army wanted this to be done to prevent the United States from spoiling its plans in Asia. The headstrong General Tojo became Prime Minister in October 1941. After obtaining a promise of help from Germany in November, he decided to attack the United States. On 7 December 1941, the Japanese navy launched a surprise sea-air raid on Pearl Harbour, Hawaii, and nearly destroyed the whole United States Pacific Fleet. The success of the operation was radioed back to Japan by the code word 'Tora!' which meant 'Tiger!'.

Brighter than the Sun

The attack on Pearl Harbour was only the first step in a bigger plan of battle. Immediately after Pearl Harbour, Japanese forces attacked Hong Kong, Singapore, Guam, the Philippines and Malaya. The Allies at war with Japan included China, the United States, Britain and the Netherlands.

At first Japanese forces were successful almost everywhere, but the combined strength and resources of the Allies made it difficult for Japan to keep up the fight. At the same time secret experiments were being made in the deserts of New Mexico. By July 1945 American scientists had made ready an atom bomb which had the same destructive power as 20000 tons of TNT explosive. An eye-witness in New Mexico, looking through a blackened piece of glass, wrote that the bomb was 'a bright ball of fire, which was far brighter than the sun'.

After the Japanese government had refused to surrender without conditions, the Americans decided to use the bomb. On

6 August an atom bomb was dropped by a B29 bomber on the industrial city of Hiroshima and destroyed the whole city of 250000 people. Ten hours later another bomb struck Nagasaki. In September 1945 Japan surrendered to the Allies.

The New Japan

Shortly before the formal surrender took place the occupation of Japan had begun. The Allies agreed that the famous General MacArthur should be appointed to carry out the work of re-construction. He was given the title of Supreme Commander of the Allied Powers or SCAP. General MacArthur brought with him 30000 officials and, working in close co-operation with Japanese officials, gradually carried out many important improvements.

In 1951 the peace treaty was finally signed with forty-eight countries in San Francisco. In the following year the period of occupation ended and Japan became an independent country once more. In 1956 she became a member of United Nations, and, in 1964, she impressed the whole world by running the Olympic Games very successfully in Tokyo. This was followed by yet another spectacular international event. In 1970 the Trade Fair at Osaka attracted millions of admiring visitors. Those events, together with rapid industrial growth and the ever-growing prosperity of her citizens showed that Japan had completely recovered from the destruction of the war.

The Trade Fair at Osaka

Two Olympic Games stamps

Things To Do

1 Describe briefly how and why Japan was re-opened to foreign trade.

2 What were the main aims of the leaders of the Meiji Restoration? Were these aims achieved by the end of the century?

3 Describe briefly how Japan became a modern power.

4 Write a short paragraph on what you know about the Japanese constitution.

5 What advantages or disadvantages did the wars of 1894–95, 1904–5 and 1914–19 bring to Japan?

6 Describe briefly how the militarists led Japan into the Second World War.

7 Collect up-to-date pictures to show how Japan has recovered from the destruction of the war.

8 Write a short sentence about each of the following to explain their meaning: Son-no Jo-i, Diet, genro, moningu, zaibatsu, Tora, SCAP

12
The Contemporary World

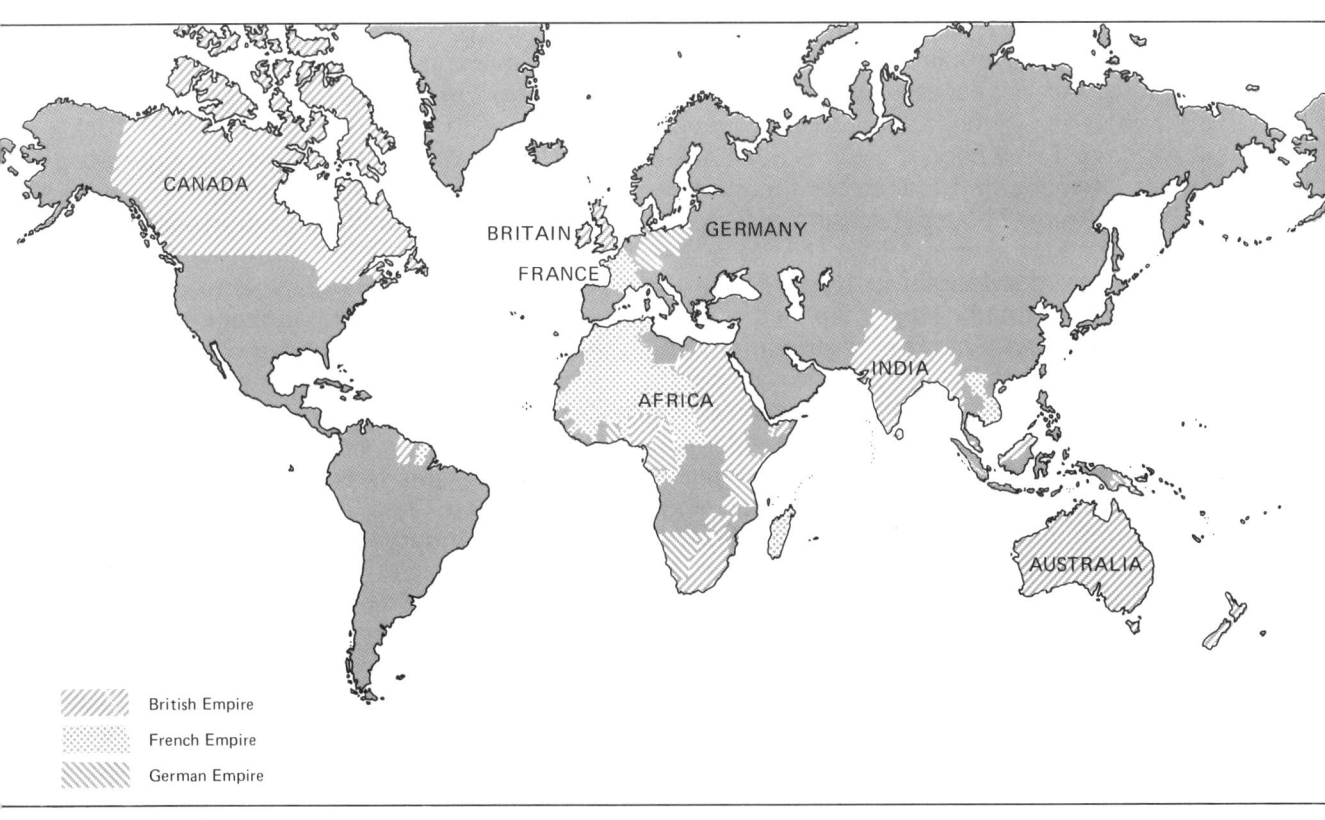

British Empire

French Empire

German Empire

Empires before 1914

In the twentieth century there have been two world wars, the first one fought mainly in Europe from 1914 to 1918, and the second one fought in many different parts of the world between the years 1939 and 1945. These wars have been terribly destructive, and men have been wondering ever since why the wars happened and how to prevent a third world war from taking place. In this chapter we will look at the alliances and rivalries between countries and will see how disagreements became major wars.

Colonial Empires before 1914

Industrial change made the European nations rich and powerful and enabled them to conquer large empires overseas because they had better guns and better-trained armies than most of the nations outside Europe. Britain, France, Holland, Germany, Portugal and Spain were the main empire builders, but Spain and Portugal had lost most of their possessions abroad due to the lack of strong naval power. Britain had a very large navy and, by the beginning of the nineteenth century, had strengthened her position as the greatest sea power. Most of her soldiers were stationed in the empire and she was not anxious to weaken her forces abroad by being drawn into quarrels in Europe.

Germany and France

By 1870 Germany was united after defeating France in the Franco-Prussian War. She strengthened her position by gaining a foot-hold in Africa and began to rival other nations as an empire builder. One reason for expansion was to enable businessmen to find new markets in which to sell their products and to obtain raw materials from countries rich in resources which Germany did not possess. France already had colonies in Africa and very soon there was rivalry be-tween Germany and France for the control of North Africa. The most serious crisis took place over Morocco in 1905. The Kaiser of Germany visited Tangier in North Africa to show that Germany was interested in ac-quiring territory. The French thought that the Germans were trying to control Morocco and were very angry. The result was a con-ference and Germany had to recognise the independence of Morocco. France later found reasons to send in troops and Morocco became a French colony; France and Germany remained on bad terms. France made an alliance with Russia.

Britain and Germany

Britain and Germany were on good terms at the beginning of the twentieth century and very nearly made an alliance. However, all thought of this vanished when they became rivals at sea. Germany began to build a big navy and Britain felt that this was a threat to her power, especially as Germany had now developed the strongest army in Europe. Nevertheless, Britain's colonial empire was much greater; Germany then turned to her neighbour, Austria-Hungary, with whom she was already allied. These two nations became known as the Central Powers. France, who was now faced with strong power on her borders, wanted an alliance with Britain, but Britain would only permit a friendly agreement, called the Entente Cordiale, which did not promise any military help in time of war, but established a better relationship between the two countries.

Austria-Hungary and Russia

The Austro-Hungarian and Russian empires contained many peoples each with their own language and customs. Most wanted their independence but were held together as long as there was peace. When war broke out, both empires collapsed and were div-ided into the countries we know today. Austria-Hungary and Russia were rivals for power in the Balkan peninsula where the old Turkish Empire was growing weaker. In 1912 and 1913 the Serbs, the Monteneg-rans, the Greeks and the Bulgarians joined together to try and win independence from Turkey. They called themselves the Balkan League. Austria-Hungary and Russia kept an eye on what was happening to ensure that things did not get out of control. They did not want an unfriendly power to control the Bosphorus straits and the Dardanelles because they were vital for trade and communication between countries.

But there was hostile feeling between Austria-Hungary and Serbia, one of the Balkan states. Serbia wanted the lands along the Dalmatian coast owned by Austria-Hungary and wanted to set free the people there who were Slavs. Serbia herself was a Slav nation and wanted to unite all Slavs. Austria-Hungary was determined to prevent Serbian ambitions. The opportunity came in 1914 when an Austrian prince was as-sassinated by a Serbian Slav: Austria de-clared war. This was the event that began the First World War.

The Austrian prince just before he was assassinated

Trench Warfare

The First World War

When the Austrians attacked Serbia, Germany promised to help Austria-Hungary, while Russia, another Slav nation, promised to help Serbia. Russia prepared to attack Austria-Hungary. Germany attacked France, Russia's ally, and sent her troops through Belgium because it was a neutral state. Britain protested, but as Germany took no notice Britain prepared to fight for Belgium and France and Russia, against Germany and Austria-Hungary. They called themselves the Allied Powers. Most people thought that the war would be a short one, but it lasted for four years and was fought on two fronts, the western front between Belgium-France and Germany, and the eastern front, between Germany, Austria-Hungary and Russia.

The war dragged on because there was no decisive victory and both sides lost many soldiers during the fighting. They also became short of supplies of guns and ammunition. Soldiers dug long ditches where they could shelter from enemy guns and could attack without being seen. This new form of battle was called 'trench warfare'. It was very muddy, cold and unpleasant.

After the first two years Germany and Austria found no further allies, but the Allied Powers were increasing in number. Eventually thirty-two allied nations were fighting against four. In 1917, however, Russia withdrew from the war because she was involved in an internal revolution. But the Allied Powers gained the support of the United States of America who, as we read in Chapter 7, joined the war because German submarines were attacking American ships. The United States of America had vast numbers of men who could be trained as soldiers and plenty of supplies of guns and ammunition as well as food. By the autumn of 1918, Germany and Austria-Hungary were so exhausted that they were willing to discuss peace terms. Both countries were on the edge of revolution.

The peace treaty of Versailles was made in France after the war. The Allied Powers decided what should happen to the German and Austro-Hungarian empires: the four empires of Russia, Austria-Hungary, Turkey and Germany were broken up; new countries such as Czechoslovakia, Poland, Yugoslavia, Estonia, Latvia, Lithuania and Finland were established; Germany lost not only territory to her neighbours but also all her colonies abroad; she also had to pay the Allied Powers for the damage they had suffered in the war. The Germans thought that this peace treaty was very harsh and unfair. Austria was reduced to a tiny state in central Europe and Hungary became completely independent.

The Russian Revolution

At the beginning of the twentieth century, Russia was ruled by an absolute monarch — the tsar. This government was inefficient. The poor land workers had few rights and most of the government officials were corrupt and ignorant. There were very few good roads, schools or factories. Then Russia was involved in a war with Japan in 1904—5 and was defeated. At that time revolutionaries began to unite and talk about the faults in the system. Matters grew more serious during the First World War. The Russians had kept up the fighting on the eastern front, but they were weakened by it. They had hardly any food, clothes or ammunition. Finally factory workers went on strike in March 1917 and joined the women in the long shopping queues. This turned into a demonstration. The Tsar, Nicholas II, ordered the military to fire on the demonstrators, but they refused and joined them instead. Soon more and more people were against the Tsar. They demanded an end to the war. By the end of the month the Tsar was forced to abdicate. He was later murdered by revolutionaries.

Control was now taken over by people of the middle class. They were influenced by the ideas of Karl Marx who wrote a book called *Das Kapital.* In this book he said that capitalist systems should be replaced by government by the working people. This was the beginning of Communism. Nicolai Lenin was a follower of Karl Marx and he took over control of the Bolsheviks. This was the name of the new party which was in power.

Russia made peace with Germany but had to fight for many more years against people who did not want Russia to be Communist. The new Bolshevik government took control of everything including industry, agriculture, transport and land. They would not allow any opposition to their ideas and many people died or went to prison or into exile because they did not agree with Communist ideas. The new Communist state of Russia wanted to encourage revolution everywhere and this made other countries very suspicious of it. Communist parties grew up in many other countries and some of them wanted to overthrow their governments too, but they were not successful in Eastern Europe until after the Second World War.

When Lenin died in 1924, there was a struggle for power among the Bolsheviks.

Lenin speaking in Red Square, Moscow

The man who took control was Joseph Stalin. He managed to get rid of his rivals and made himself very powerful in Russia until his death in 1953. He was greatly feared. Stalin was responsible for the five-year plans which were the basis of Russian economy.

The League of Nations

We read in Chapter 7 how President Wilson helped to set up an international organisation to try and solve disputes between nations without war. It was called the League of Nations and met in Geneva, Switzerland. Representatives of most of the Allied Powers and neutral nations met here to discuss international problems such as what should be done with refugees. These were people who had to leave their countries for political reasons. The League of Nations set up committees to investigate diseases and to find ways of improving agriculture in backward countries.

During the 1920s the League of Nations was quite successful in settling disputes between member countries. Finland and Sweden settled a quarrel about a group of islands in the Baltic Sea. Greece and Bulgaria were prevented from going to war over a frontier dispute. During the 1930s the League of Nations was not so successful because the problems were more serious and concerned more powerful nations such as Italy and Germany. When Italy attacked Abyssinia, the League could not prevent it. Nor could it do anything when Germany marched her soldiers into the Rhineland frontier area where she was not supposed to keep any soldiers. At the outbreak of the Second World War in 1939, the League of Nations found itself powerless to prevent another war.

League of Nations Mandates

After the First World War Germany and Turkey had to give up all their colonial territories and their empires. These territories were put under the care of the Allied Powers

The League of Nations buildings in Geneva

Stalin

as League of Nations Mandates. The Allied Powers were to administer the mandates for the League of Nations until the mandates could become independent nations. Germany's empire in Africa was put under the control of Britain and South Africa, and her colonies in the Pacific were put under the control of Australia. Turkey's empire in the Middle East was put under the control of Britain and France.

League of Nations Mandates were less successful with larger states. When Palestine became a British mandate both the Jews and the Arabs hoped that it would one day become their state and both groups prepared for this. Soon there was fighting between the Jews and the Arabs and no peaceful solution could be found until after the Second World War when the state of Israel was created for the Jews.

Mussolini

During the First World War, Italy fought with the Allied Powers. At the Peace Conference, she was given some Austrian territories but many Italians wanted more. In particular they wanted the Dalmatian coast which formed part of Yugoslavia. There was much poverty and unemployment in Italy after the war and many people began to listen to a young man called Benito Mussolini who said that Italy should not accept the Treaty of Versailles but should try to conquer the land she wanted. His followers were called Fascists. In 1922 Mussolini became Prime Minister of Italy and soon made Italy a Fascist state, which he ruled strictly. He was a dictator. There were improvements in roads, many new public buildings and more jobs for the people, so most people accepted the new government although there was no freedom of speech and no democracy.

True to his promise that Italy should expand, Mussolini attacked Abyssinia in East Africa in 1935. The Italians had tried once before to conquer Abyssinia but had failed. This time in 1935, they had good weapons and soon defeated the Abyssinians, and they then made the country an Italian colony.

A Nazi meeting

Hitler

Hitler was an Austrian who came to live in Germany after fighting in the German army during the First World War. He was a very persuasive speaker and soon had many followers who agreed with his ideas. He told them that the Treaty of Versailles which had ended the war was unfair to Germany, and that the Germans had not really lost the war, but had been tricked by the Allies. One of Hitler's ideas was that the Germans were a superior race of people and that other races were inferior and some of them should be destroyed. These other 'races' included Catholics, Muslims and Jews, but he persecuted the Jews first. There were many Jews living in Austria and Germany at this time and Hitler's followers were jealous of their wealth and positions of responsibility. Hitler's followers were called

Mussolini

130

Nazis, or National Socialists, and they became an important political group in Germany. In 1923 they tried to seize power in Munich, a town in southern Germany, but they failed and Hitler was put in prison for a short time. There he wrote a book called *Mein Kampf* (My Struggle) in which he wrote about the glory that Germany could achieve.

The Nazis Take Power

In 1929 there was a very bad financial crisis, which began in New York. Shops, banks, factories and other places of work had to close, so many people were unemployed both in Germany and in most other countries in Europe. This was called the Depression and lasted for several years. In Germany more and more people listened to Hitler because he promised that Germany would be great again and that people would have work and enough to eat. Hitler was elected Chancellor of Germany in 1933 and he very soon changed Germany into a Nazi dictatorship by taking complete control himself. He called himself the *Führer* which means 'Leader'. He immediately increased the army and built up a strong navy. He prepared to attack any country which opposed his plans. At home he began to persecute the Jews and anyone else who opposed him. These people were arrested, sometimes shot and sometimes sent to concentration camps where they had to work terribly hard for very little food, and often died from the bad conditions. Hitler later decided to get rid of the Jews by killing them in special concentration camps. It is thought that about six million Jews died in these camps.

The Second World War

Hitler made an alliance with Mussolini, and, for a short time, with Russia. Together they conquered most of the countries in Western Europe. They occupied France, Belgium, Holland, Denmark, Norway, Poland and Czechoslovakia. Hitler tried to attack Britain, but his Air Force was weaker than the British Air Force so he changed his plans.

A German concentration camp

In Britain the Prime Minister, Winston Churchill, encouraged the people never to surrender to Hitler but to continue fighting whatever the cost. He told the members of Parliament that he could offer nothing but 'blood, toil, tears and sweat' and he said that his government's aim was 'to wage war by sea, land and air, war with all our minds and with all the strength that God gives us'.

In the Far East, Hitler had an alliance with Japan, who wanted to expand her power over Asia. In 1941 Japan attacked Pearl

Mussolini and Hitler during the war

Harbour, the United States naval base at Hawaii in the central Pacific Ocean. This made the United States join the war on the side of Britain and the Allies against Japan and Germany. An alliance was made between the United States of America, Britain and Russia, to fight against Germany, Italy and Japan. The Americans dropped two atom bombs on the Japanese cities, Hiroshima and Nagasaki. The bombs completely destroyed these towns and the Japanese were forced to surrender. The United States occupied Japan for five years after the war as we read in Chapter 7. Italy gradually recovered after the war and became a republic. Germany was occupied by the United States, Britain, France and Russia. Unfortunately they could not agree about the future of Germany because Russia wanted Germany to be a Communist state, but the other three nations did not want this to happen. So Germany was divided into a Communist East Germany, and non-Communist West Germany. The city of Berlin, the old capital, was divided into two. The Communists built a wall to prevent Germans escaping from the East to the West.

The first atom bomb explosion

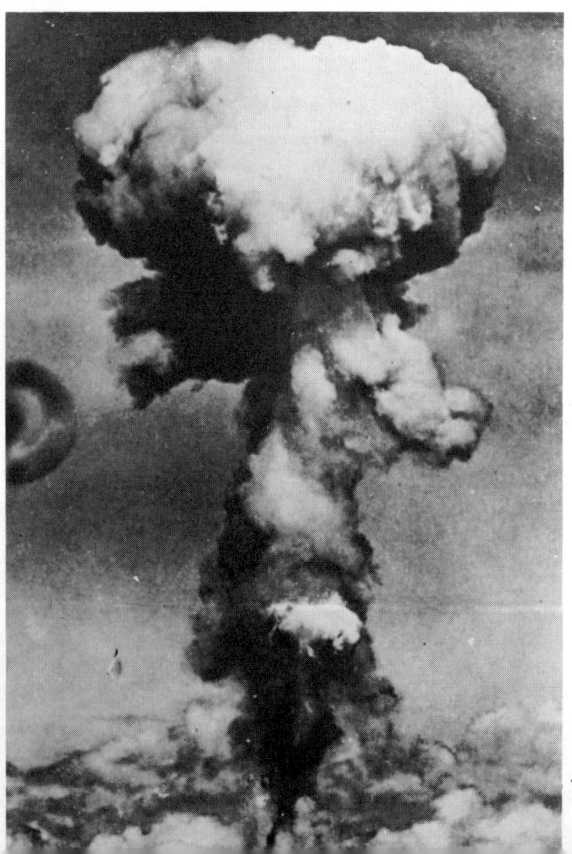

The Growth of Communism

In the countries in Europe and Asia which were conquered by Germany or Japan, there were underground movements of people who wanted to attack the invaders. These were usually led by Communists, and after the war was over, they prepared to take over the country and make it a Communist state. This happened in Eastern Europe in Poland, Hungary, Czechoslovakia, Romania, Bulgaria, Yugoslavia and the Baltic States of Latvia, Lithuania and Estonia. They were encouraged by Russia who wanted these countries to be Communist and to accept Russian leadership. Yugoslavia managed to become a Communist country without being under Russian influence. Marshal Tito was the leader responsible for this. But Hungary and Czechoslovakia who made similar attempts to break free of Russia were put down by Russian troops.

In the Far East the Communists fought a civil war in China against the Nationalists; the Communists, led by Mao Tse Tung, were successful in driving the Nationalists out of mainland China into Taiwan. The Communists in China encouraged Communists in Korea and Malaya and Indo-China to try to make their countries Communist. Korea and Vietnam were both divided into a northern Communist state and a southern non-Communist state, but Malaya remained non-Communist. The Communists continued their efforts in the other countries of Indo-China, Thailand, Laos and Cambodia. Many world problems today spring from Communist expansion in the Far East. It is important to remember that one of the aims of Communism is that all countries in the world will eventually have a Communist government.

The United Nations

After the Second World War another international organisation was set up to prevent further wars. It was called the United Nations and the representatives of the nations met in New York. The United Nations has far more members than the League ever had, including the United States of America, which

The United Nations building in New York

had not been a member of the League. The United Nations can ask member nations to provide soldiers so that a United Nations force can be sent to keep peace between two quarrelling nations. The League was not able to do this. But the United Nations cannot interfere unless the countries concerned are members of the United Nations and actually ask for help.

Things To Do

1 Using the map of Colonial Territories in 1914, list the colonies of each of the European powers. Compare this with a recent atlas map and note which countries have become independent and whether they have changed their names.

2 List the nations who fought in the First World War on each side and compare this with those who fought in the Second World War.

3 Explain briefly why the Germans did not like the Peace Treaty made after the First World War.

4 Look up the following people in an encyclopaedia and make brief notes about them:

Lenin	Mussolini
Stalin	Mao Tse-tung
Hitler	Winston Churchill

5 Hold a discussion on Hitler's leadership. Why do you think he rose to power? Try to talk to older people who lived at the same time.

6 Make a class project on the United Nations. You should have sections on its history, its present-day work and a study on one of its leaders.

13
Scientific and Cultural Developments

Ford Model 'T' car

A German Zeppelin

The Wright brothers and their aircraft

Road Transport

Modern land transport depends on the petrol engine which was invented in the late nineteenth century, but cars were not in general use until the twentieth century. Motor buses and lorries began to replace horse buses and carts during the first ten years of the twentieth century, and armoured cars and tanks were first used in the First World War. After the war, cars were manufactured by mass production and could be sold more cheaply so that ordinary people could afford to buy them. The Austin 7 was first produced in 1922 and cost £165. In America the Ford Model T was very popular. In the country tractors were invented to draw farm machinery. Since that time the design of all these motor vehicles has changed many times and they have become faster and more powerful. It has become so useful to own a car that there are serious traffic problems in many cities throughout the world.

The invention and use of motor vehicles meant that roads had to be improved. At first solid rubber tyres were used, but soon inflatable ones were preferred which meant that road surfaces had to be much smoother. Road surfaces began to be made of small stones coated with tar, or of concrete. They had to be repaired and re-made quite often.

Air Travel

Many people tried to invent flying machines, some of which were designed like birds' wings. But until balloons were invented in the eighteenth century no one managed to be airborne. In 1783 a hydrogen balloon made an ascent in Paris; during the siege of Paris nearly one hundred years later, in 1870, several people escaped from Paris by balloon. During the First World War the Germans used large balloons, called Zeppelins, which they sent over England to drop bombs, but they were so big that they were very easy to shoot down, and they were also difficult to control.

The first successful aeroplane was made by the Wright brothers in the United States in 1903. In 1909 a young Frenchman, called Blériot, crossed the English Channel by aeroplane. In 1919 two English officers crossed the Atlantic and after this it soon became possible for people to travel from place to place by aeroplane. Although aeroplanes were not used very much in the First World War except for spying, by the Second World War aeroplanes played a major part in both attack and defence.

Since the Second World War jet engines have been invented which has made air travel very much faster. Guided missiles make it possible to attack a far distant city or to attack an aeroplane in the sky before it has reached its destination.

One of the most convenient modern forms of transport for peace or war is the helicopter, which was invented after the Second World War.

Scientific research in air travel has recently made tremendous progress. It was discovered that by shooting off a missile with a rocket it would go out of the earth's atmosphere and into orbit. The Russians were the first to achieve this remarkable feat in 1957 and, in 1961, Yuri Gagarin, also a Russian, became the first man in space. The Americans have made as much progress as the Russians and in 1969 they put the first man on the moon. Other planets will soon be explored. One of the practical uses of these space satellites is to transmit television and telephone waves.

Firing a space rocket into orbit

Sea Transport

Sea transport has not developed quite so fast in the twentieth century though there have been many technical improvements. Steamships were invented in the nineteenth century and have been made faster and more efficient. Submarines were developed by the Germans who used them in the First World War to attack British and French shipping and did much damage. By the Second World War large ships called aircraft carriers had been built so that aeroplanes could fly at sea. Since the war hydrofoils have been developed and travel much faster than most ships, skimming across the water on fins. Hovercraft actually travel over the surface of the water. These have speeded up sea transport over short distances, but long distances still have to be travelled by steamship. Nuclear power has been used for submarines and will perhaps be more widely used in the future.

A model of Apollo II landing on the moon in 1970

Medical Knowledge

During the twentieth century remarkable developments have taken place in medicine and many terrible diseases, which in the past caused many deaths, can now be prevented or cured. X-rays can be used to discover various diseases, such as tuberculosis, long before there is any outward sign. Vaccination can prevent smallpox while inoculation prevents cholera. Anaesthetics can deaden the nerves in part of the body, or put a person to sleep so that no pain is felt during an operation. Much longer and more complicated operations can now be performed. Doctors can now take an organ from the body of one person and put it in the body of another. This is called transplanting and has been done with the kidney and the heart.

Handicapped people, such as the deaf and the blind and those who have lost the use of a leg or an arm, can now be helped with such devices as hearing aids, a machine which can help a blind person to 'see' by using sound waves, and artificial limbs. There is a great deal of research going on in many countries to help handicapped people live as normal a life as possible.

Some diseases, such as leprosy, used to be considered so terrible that the people who had the disease had to live away from the rest of society. Medical research has discovered that many diseases can be cured by drugs and that operations can be performed to help people who have lost the use of one of their limbs.

Entertainment

During the twentieth century people have become used to the cinema and television for their entertainment. Moving films were first invented at the beginning of the century and became very popular after the First World War; one of the most famous of the early film stars was Charlie Chaplin. At first the films were silent and a pianist was hired to play music to go with the film. Quite soon sound was added to the film and, later, colour. After the Second World War, television made its appearance and made it

Charlie Chaplin in the film The Kid

possible for people to stay at home and watch films instead of going out to the cinema.

The radio was invented in the late nineteenth century but did not come into common use until after the First World War. It became useful not only for entertainment but also for communication with ships at sea and for police and for the army. It has become the quickest way for any government to inform its people of world affairs or to tell them what to do in an emergency. During the Second World War many people living in countries, such as France, Belgium and Holland, occupied by Germany, were able to listen secretly to the English radio and even to receive messages.

Modern Art

One of the most famous artists of the twentieth century is Pablo Picasso who was born in Spain but has lived most of his life in France. He uses many styles of painting but became famous before the First World War for his paintings in the Cubist style. Cubists reduced everything to geometric shapes. Later his paintings became more realistic again. In 1937 a small village called Guernica

Picasso's painting: Guernica

was bombed during the Spanish Civil War and Picasso was so horrified that he painted a black and white picture to show the horror of bombing. You can see the picture on this page.

After the First World War many painters began to paint ideas from dreams and a new style called Surrealism was born. They tried to paint exactly as the thoughts came to them as if in a dream world. The best known of these painters is probably Salvador Dali who paints many rather frightening pictures. He, too, painted one about the Spanish Civil War as well as a number of strange religious pictures.

In the early 1920s, a group of artists and sculptors began to meet together in Germany trying to unify the arts. They were called the Bauhaus group and among them were the painters Kandinsky and Klee and the architect Gropius. They produced some remarkable works of art and influenced many artists. Art-teaching today has been very much influenced by the Bauhaus ideas.

Artists and architects have tried to experiment in every way possible and sometimes their results have been unfortunate, but they have made people think more about the use and value of art.

Music

Two of the greatest composers and musicians of the twentieth century were Stravinsky and Bartok. Stravinsky was born in Russia and wrote music for a famous Russian Ballet group under the direction of Diaghilev. His most famous ballet music was Petrushka written in 1911. It was the story of a puppet theatre and the feelings of the puppets. His music is dramatic and exciting.

After the First World War a new form of music became popular — jazz. It developed first among the black people living in the city of New Orleans, United States of America, from the songs and dances popular among them, but soon it was copied and imitated by people all over the world. It proved to be wonderful music to dance to and was a great change from the more formal

The ballet Petrushka

waltzes and ballroom dances of the pre-war period. One of the greatest jazz musicians was Louis Armstrong. The slow, sad rhythms became known as 'the Blues' and the more energetic numbers as 'Dixieland'. Jazz depended greatly on improvisation, that is, playing without written music but following a general theme or idea in the music.

Since the Second World War other forms of popular music have developed such as rock-and-roll and folk music, but jazz is still enjoyed.

The invention of sound recording has meant that great musicians and singers will never be forgotten because their records can be played long after they are dead.

Costume

Changes in costume reflect social and political developments closely. Before the First World War it was easy to tell the rich from the poor by the style as well as the material of the clothes they wore. Rich ladies wore dresses to the ground and tight corsets to pull in their waists and enormous hats when they went out. This made it almost impossible to do any hard, manual work. When one lady bravely wore wide, baggy trousers (bloomers) in order to ride a bicycle, many people were very shocked. During the First World War, however, women began to do many jobs that men had done before because the men had gone to fight. As a result they began to wear shorter skirts and more practical clothes. After the war their skirts went up to knee length and dresses were straight with no waist. It was fashionable at the time to have very short hair so that women looked like boys. During this time men's clothes did not change so dramatically, except that trousers varied in width and fashions in hats changed.

In the 1930s women's clothes became more feminine; skirts became longer and hair was worn longer. This fashion continued through the Second World War until the 1950s when skirts began to go up and up. In the sixties mini-skirts came into fashion, and in the seventies people tried to combine longer midi skirts with 'hot pants'.

One interesting post-Second-World-War

Ladies wearing bloomers

change has been the way women have worn trousers more and more until they have become just as fashionable and acceptable as skirts. Another recent change is the increasing interest in men's clothes. Brighter colours and more interesting materials are being used and men are growing their hair longer until they look almost like the men at the beginning of the twentieth century. Each fashion copies a particular fashion of the past and tries to make it a little different. With modern communications and newspapers, people all over the world copy the fashions so national variety is becoming less and less.

Things To Do

1 Write an illustrated project on two of the following:

    land transport   air transport
    sea transport   space travel

Trace their development in the twentieth century and collect pictures from the newspapers of the most recent examples.

2 Write a review of a film you have seen recently.

3 Visit an art gallery or picture exhibition and write a brief account.

4 Listen to music by one of the composers mentioned and write your impressions.

5 Study twentieth-century fashion for men and women and draw some of the most recent fashions. Imagine the fashions of the future.

6 Find out how a radio is made.

7 Look critically at some modern buildings in your area. Say which is the best and which is the ugliest and give your reasons.

Top left *Fashions in the 1920s*

Top right *A 1930 fashion plate*

Left *Chandigah in India: A building designed by Le Corbusier*

Above A Garden at Night. *A modern painting by Paul Klee*

Below *Salvador Dali:* Metamorphosis of Narcissus.
This is a Surrealist painting

INDEX Index

A

Abahai 101
Aborigines 59
Abyssinia (see Ethiopia)
Adam, Robert 53
Agricultural Revolution 48, 49
Alamo, Battle of the 67
Alexander I 41
Alexander II 41
Alexander III 42
Algeria 37, 63
Allied Powers 127, 128, 129, 130
American Civil War 73, 88
American Revolution, The 58, 86
Amherst 109
Anglo-Japanese Alliance 121
Angola 90
Annam 10, 11, 93, 94
Apartheid 62
Arabs 82, 85, 92
Arkwright, Richard 46
Ashikaga Takauji 15, 16
Atom bomb 122
Australia 57, 59
Austria 38, 126, 127
Axum 84
Azuchi 17

B

Bakewell, Robert 49
Balkan League 126
Balkans 24, 40
Baltic Sea 24
Bangladesh 60
Banners 101
Bastille 39
Belgian Congo 90
Berbers 82, 83
Berlin 132
Bermuda 58
Biddle 113
Bismarck 38, 89
Black Sea 24
Blériot 135
Boers 62
Boleyn, Anne 24
Bolsheviks 120, 128
Bonaparte, Napoléon 29, 35, 36, 55, 66
Borneo 11, 61, 96
Boston 58
Boulton, Matthew 47
Bourgeoisie 29

Boxer Protocol 111
Boxers 111
British East India Company 60, 61, 94, 107
Brooke, James 61, 96
Brunel, Isambard Kingdom 48
Burma, 57, 60, 93, 94
Bushido 20

C

Cairo 83, 89
California 67, 68
Cambaluc 3, 5, 6, 7
Cambodia 11, 37, 93, 94, 95
Canada 57, 58
Canton 10, 109
Canton System 108
Capetown 89
Carthage 82
Castro, Fidel 77
Catapult 3
Cathay 4, 5
Catherine of Aragon 24
Catherine the Great 30
Cavour 39
Central Powers 126
Ceylon 11, 60
Charles I 26
Charles II 27, 45
Charles X 37
Charleston 75
Charter Oath 117
Cheng Ho 10, 11, 92
Chiang Kai-shek 112
Chin 1, 101
Ch'ien-lung 104, 107, 110
Chinese Communist Party 112
Ch'ing 101, 104, 109, 110
Chonin 22, 23
Civil Service Examinations 8
Chosu 115, 117, 118
Chu Hsi 103
Chu Ti (see Yung-lo)
Chu Yüan-chang (see Hung-wu)
Ch'üan-chou 5, 10
Chulalongkorn 93, 94
Church of England 25
Churchill, Winston 131
Civil Rights Movement 75
Cleveland 76
Code Napoléon 35
Columbus 5, 92
Commonwealth 27, 57, 62
Communist Manifesto 38
Communism 96, 128, 132
Confederacy 74
Confucius 8

International Working Men's Association 38
Islam 82, 84
Israel 130
Italy 24
Ito 117, 120
I-t'ung chih 9

J
James II 27
Japan 10, 11
Java 10, 11
Jefferson, Thomas 66
Jesuits 17, 26
Johnson, Andrew 75
Johnson, President 75

K
Kabuki 22
Kaifeng 1
Kamakura 15
K'ang-hsi 102, 103, 104
Karakorum 2
Kennedy, President J F 75, 77, 79
Kenya 63
Kerulen River 2
Khanate 3
Koran 84
Korea 5, 10, 11, 16, 18, 101, 119
Kossuth 39
Koxinga 102
Kuang-hsü 111
Kublai Khan 3, 7, 15
Kwantung Army 121
Kyoto 15, 16, 21, 115

L
Laos 37, 95
Law of the Military Houses 20
Laxman 113
League of Nations 78, 79, 90, 129, 130
Lee, General Robert E 75
Lee Kuan Yew 98
Lenin, Nicolai 42, 128
Leopold II 89
Li Shih-chen 10
Li Tzu-ch'eng 11, 101
Liao 1
Liaotung 100
Liberia 86, 87
Light, Captain 95
Lincoln, Abraham 74
Lisbon 84
Liu-chius 10
Livingstone, David 87, 88
Lombardy 39
London Missionary Society 87

Louis XIV 28
Louis XVI 29
Louis XVIII 37
Louis Philippe 37
Louis Napoléon 37
Louisiana Purchase 67
Luther, Martin 24

M
Macao 18, 19, 92
MacArthur, General 123
Macartney 108
Magellan 93
Malacca 10, 11, 61, 92, 95
Malawi 62
Malaya 61, 98
Malaysia 97
Mali 83
Manchuria 1
Manchus 11, 42, 100, 110
Mansa Musa 83
Mao Tse-tung 112, 132
Maoris 59
Marx, Karl 38, 42, 128
Maryland 58
Mazzini 39
Meiji 115, 116, 118, 120
Mein Kampf 131
Metternich, Prince 38
Mexican War, The 67
Mexico 68, 93
Ming 7, 11, 100, 101, 102
Missouri, River 67
Modena 39
Moldavia and Wallachia 40
Mongols 4, 5, 8, 11, 15, 101, 104
Mongolia 2
Mongut 93, 94
Mormons 73
Morocco 37, 63, 82, 84, 126
Mozambique 90
Mozart, Wolfgang Amadeus 54
Mukden 101
Muromochi 16
Muskets 17, 18
Muslims 4, 11, 82
Mussolini, Benito 130

N
Nagasaki 19, 20, 23, 79, 113, 123, 132
Nanking 8
Naples 38
Napoléon I (see Bonaparte)
Napoléon III (see Louis)
Nara 16
Nazis 131

10.50
net

40H82J